Winged Messengers

THE DECLINE OF BIRDS

HOWARD YOUTH

Thomas Prugh, *Editor*

WORLDWATCH PAPER 165

THE WORLDWATCH INSTITUTE is an independent research organization that works for an environmentally sustainable and socially just society, in which the needs of all people are met without threatening the health of the natural environment or the well-being of future generations. By providing compelling, accessible, and fact-based analysis of critical global issues, Worldwatch informs people around the world about the complex interactions among people, nature, and economies. Worldwatch focuses on the underlying causes of and practical solutions to the world's problems, in order to inspire people to demand new policies, investment patterns, and lifestyle choices.

FINANCIAL SUPPORT for the Institute is provided by the Aria Foundation, the Richard & Rhoda Goldman Fund, The George Gund Foundation, The William and Flora Hewlett Foundation, The Frances Lear Foundation, The John D. and Catherine T. MacArthur Foundation, the Merck Family Fund, the Curtis and Edith Munson Foundation, Nalith, Inc., the NIB Foundation, The Overbrook Foundation, The David and Lucile Packard Foundation, The Shared Earth Foundation, The Shenandoah Foundation, Turner Foundation, Inc., the UN Environment Programme, the Wallace Global Fund, the Weeden Foundation, and The Winslow Foundation. The Institute also receives financial support from its Council of Sponsors members Adam and Rachel Albright, Tom and Cathy Crain, John and Laurie McBride and Kate McBride Puckett, Robert Wallace and Raisa Scriabine, and from the many other friends of Worldwatch.

THE WORLDWATCH PAPERS provide in-depth, quantitative, and qualitative analysis of the major issues affecting prospects for a sustainable society. The Papers are written by members of the Worldwatch Institute research staff or outside specialists and are reviewed by experts unaffiliated with Worldwatch. They have been used as concise and authoritative references by governments, nongovernmental organizations, and educational institutions worldwide. For a partial list of available Worldwatch Papers, go online to www.worldwatch.org/pubs/paper.

Contents

Figure, Tables, and Boxes

Acknowledgments: Special thanks to Linda Starke, Chris Flavin, Gary Gardner, and Chris Bright for providing the spark that set this project alight. Editor Tom Prugh deserves special praise for tackling with skill and grace a manuscript that bound together so many once-scattered thoughts. Thanks again go to Linda Starke as well as Ed Ayres for their refinements to my previous works on birds, which provided a springboard for this publication. Brian Halweil, Lisa Mastny, and other Worldwatch colleagues also provided valued and fresh input and information, while Radhika Sarin sent crucial reference materials to me in "far off" Spain. Art director Lyle Rosbotham made it all look good, and I'm grateful to Leanne Mitchell, Susan Finkelpearl, and Susanne Martikke for their outreach expertise, and to Elizabeth Nolan for her astute marketing of the paper.

For advice, information, and review, I owe a debt of gratitude to Alison J. Stattersfield and Nigel Collar at BirdLife International in Cambridge, England. Ragupathy Kannan at University of Arkansas (Fort Smith), years after pointing me in the right direction for hornbills in South India, came through with some important sources that otherwise I would have missed. Also, special thanks to Emilio Escudero, librarian at SEO/BirdLife's natural history library in Madrid. In Washington, D.C., heartfelt thanks to Martha Rosen, Alvin Hutchinson, and Courtney Ann Shaw at the Smithsonian Institution's natural history libraries.

With deep gratitude, I thank my patient, loving wife Marta, who never tires of reading my drafts and who shares my love for feathered creatures, and my parents, who always encouraged me to do what I love—to learn more about the natural world.

Howard Youth has researched and written for Worldwatch Institute publications for more than a decade, starting when he was Associate Editor for *World Watch* from 1989 to 1992. Fueled by a life-long interest in wildlife, he has written about conservation issues as a co-author of *State of the World 2003* and *Vital Signs*, and for *World Watch*. He has published extensively on conservation issues in other publications as well, including *National Wildlife*, *Wildlife Conservation*, and *The Washington Post*. Youth previously worked for the National Zoological Park's support group Friends of the National Zoo (FONZ), where he was an editor and communications manager. An ardent birder since age 12, he has spotted more than 1,500 bird species on five continents.

SUMMARY

Declining bird populations signal disturbing global changes. Almost 1,200 species—about 12 percent of the world's 9800 bird species—may face extinction within the next century. Although many face multiple threats and some bird extinctions seem imminent, many can be avoided by a deep commitment to bird conservation as part of a sustainable development strategy.

People have long been inspired by the beauty, song, and varied behavior of birds. Today, we also recognize that birds provide critical goods and services in their habitats, including seed dispersal, insect and rodent control, scavenging, and pollination. In addition, many bird species are valuable environmental indicators, warning us of impending environmental problems through their waning or flourishing populations. Some help indicate acidified waters, others chemical contamination, disease, and the effects of climate warming, for example.

Human-related factors threaten 99 percent of the most imperiled bird species, and bird extinctions already far exceed the natural rate of loss. At least 128 species have vanished over the past 500 years, 103 of them since 1800. But extinction is only the last stage in a spiraling degeneration that sends a species into decline. A species stops functioning in its critical capacity well before the end.

During the 20th century, the human population mushroomed, while industries, cities, and international commerce exploded and wilderness areas were carved into patchworks. Habitat loss is now the single greatest overall threat to birds. Conservationists recognize the importance of protecting large, non-fragmented "source" areas, which produce surplus birds that may later help repopulate more stressed "sink" areas. Birds with small distributions especially need such large reserves.

Exotic, or non-native, species are the second greatest threat to birds. They include bird-eating brown tree snakes, rats, cats, mongooses, introduced pathogens, exotic birds that compete with natives, and introduced insects that destroy birds' forest habitats. Exotic plants also alter the local flora, with serious consequences for birds. Controlling exotic species often requires costly active management that may include pesticides and other tools that might harm native fauna as well.

Humanity also directly exploits birds. Poorly regulated or illegal hunting and capture lead to unsustainable killing of millions of birds in nations such as Malta and China. Deep-forest birds such as Neotropical* curassows and Asian pheasants quickly disappear when hunters invade pristine areas.

Paradoxically, birds can be loved to death as well. Almost a third of the world's 330 parrot species are threatened with extinction due to pressures from collecting for the pet trade, combined with habitat loss. Another form of exploitation, longline fishing, claims hundred of thousands of seabirds, which are inadvertently hooked on baited lines and then drowned. At least 23 species now face extinction from this industry. More than 30 countries have longline fleets, yet little has been done to address the problem despite findings that simple mitigation measures can drastically cut bird bycatch.

Oil spills also claim many birds. Increased tanker traffic, aging vessels, and lax regulation make the business of transporting oil hazardous. On land, oil and natural gas exploration, extraction, and pipelines threaten some of the world's most bird-rich habitats in countries such as Peru and Ecuador.

Birds face many chemical and pollution threats. For example, PCBs likely disrupt birds' endocrine systems and compro-

---

* The Neotropical faunal region encompasses southern Mexico, the West Indies, and South and Central America. It boasts many distinct species because of its isolation during the Tertiary Period (roughly 65 million to 1.8 million years ago).

mise their ability to attract mates. Pesticides kill millions of birds and weaken others, and kill off their prey, while herbicides destroy their habitats. Few countries strictly limit the use of even the more potent chemicals. Lead from spent hunters' shot, left in wetlands and swallowed by feeding birds, kills millions of waterfowl. (Recent bans in some countries are now preventing millions of those deaths.) Lead sinkers left by anglers pose one of the gravest threats to diving birds such as loons.

Skyscrapers, communications towers, and power lines can kill millions of migrating birds. Global warming, another human-made threat, poses dangers of its own. Some temperate birds seem to be changing their habits, while others that are not may be out of sync with natural processes. Bird habitats will likely change, and conservationists will have to think of landscapes and protections as much more dynamic than in the past. Some localized species might be lost when their habitat changes and they have nowhere to go.

Efforts to restore compromised habitats or lost wild species have had mixed results. Such efforts can be surprisingly complicated and lead to unintended results. Much more study is required, but many species do not have much time. Their habitats must be saved soon or they will be lost. Conservationists are identifying the world's most important bird hotspots, aided by growing ranks of amateur bird-watchers.

Community, corporate, and government involvement in varied conservation efforts will be required to elevate biodiversity and bird conservation to a higher status. Fortunately, enterprise and environmentalism seem increasingly compatible. Habitat-friendly agricultural programs provide examples, as do corporate bir-conservation efforts and the ecotourism industry, operators of which are reaching out more to communities near bird-rich habitats. Regional initiatives to combine protected areas with areas open to sustainable industries show promise for large-scale conservation. In the end, combinations of conservation efforts, responsive to local needs, must prevail. As we work toward a more sustainable future, keeping an eye on the world's birds will help us keep ourselves in check—if we are wise enough to heed the warnings.

Introduction

Fossils reveal that white storks appeared sometime during the Miocene Epoch, between 24 million and 5 million years ago—long before humans, pesticides, power lines, and firearms. The leggy, black-winged birds stalked open, grassy areas and wetlands teeming with insects, frogs, fish, rodents, and other small animals. Over millennia, storks thrived, piling their stick nests on village rooftops. In Europe, villagers wove the graceful, pest-eating birds into lore and legend as baby-carriers and harbingers of good luck. To the south, African villagers called them "grasshopper birds" or "locust birds" because stork flocks snap up the crop-devastating insects while wintering in Africa's Sahel region.[1]*

The white stork's fortunes plunged during the 20th century. Food-rich pastures, fallow fields, and wetlands gave way to pesticide-sprayed, intensively managed "modern" farmland that could not sustain the birds. Expanding power line networks added fatal collisions and electrocution to their woes, becoming the greatest direct cause of their mortality in Europe, while in Africa many migrating storks were shot or otherwise caught for food. By the 1980s, white stork populations were declining in all of the Western European countries where they nest.[2]

Over the last decade, though, white stork populations have rebounded, and scientists can't say exactly why. Many biologists suspect the recent wet Sahelian winters. Few believe,

---

* Endnotes are grouped by section and begin on page 51.

however, that storks can have a secure future without careful conservation. The fragile Sahelian plains are becoming degraded from overgrazing and over-hunting, and given the unpredictability of moisture there, along with possible adverse effects of climate change and the other threats mentioned above, the white stork's rebound in the 1990s may prove to be a brief upturn in a long-term decline.[3]

Commuting between continents, white storks respect no political boundaries. They nest, migrate through, or winter in roughly 80 nations. The species' vulnerability, and the international cooperation needed to ensure its survival, exemplify the challenges and promise of future bird (and biodiversity) conservation efforts.[4] The stork's story also highlights how much remains to be learned about the world's feathered creatures, even those that are supposedly well known.

Across the globe, human populations, pollution, temperatures, and introductions of exotic (non-native) species are generally on the rise. Meanwhile, wildlife habitats and water supplies are waning. These trends echo through many bird populations, signaling disturbing global changes. Many of the world's 9,800 bird species are flagging as they struggle against a deadly mixture of often human-caused threats. According to a 2000 study published by a global alliance of conservation organizations called BirdLife International, almost 1,200 species—about 12 percent of the world's remaining bird species—may face extinction within the next century. (See Table 1, p. 10.) Although some bird extinctions now seem imminent, many species can still be saved provided we commit to bird conservation as an integral part of a sustainable development strategy. For many reasons, such a commitment would be in humanity's best interests.[5]

Humanity has long drawn inspiration from the beauty, song, and varied behavior of birds. Through the ages, many people believed birds had magical powers and brought good (or bad) luck. Others saw them as guardians, creators, winged oracles, fertility symbols, or guides for spirits and deities. Central America's Mayas and Aztecs worshipped Quetzalcoatl, a dominant spiritual character cloaked in the iridescent green

TABLE 1

Conservation Status of the World's Bird Species, 2000

Status	Species	Percent of Total
Extinct in the wild	3	0.03
Critically endangered	182	1.9
Endangered	321	3.3
Vulnerable	680	6.9
Near-threatened	727	7.4
No threatened status	7,884	80.5
Total	9,797	

Note: Many widespread species that fall under the "no threatened status" category nonetheless are undergoing widespread declines. This categorization is by BirdLife International using the Red List classification scheme developed by the World Conservation Union.

Source: See Endnote 5 for this section.

feathers of the resplendent quetzal, a bird now sought by binocular-toting bird-watchers.[6] Ancient Egyptians similarly revered the falcon god Horus and the sacred ibis. Many cultures around the world still ascribe strong spiritual powers to birds, as well as deriving protein and ornaments from them.[7] Native American tribes still incorporate eagle feathers into their rituals, while East African pastoral tribes do the same with ostrich feathers. We also revere birds' flying abilities. Mariners once released ravens and doves aloft in hopes that the birds would steer them toward land, and marveled at the astonishing gliding ability of the albatross. Inventors, inspired by birds' flight, developed flying machines. Worldwide, artists, authors, and photographers continue to focus their energies on birds, their feathers, and flight.[8]

   In habitats around the globe, birds also provide invaluable goods and services. Scientists are just now starting to quantify these behind-the-scenes contributions. Many birds, for example, feed on fruits, scattering seeds as they feed or in their droppings as they flap from place to place. Recent studies revealed that black-casqued, brown-cheeked, and piping hornbills are among tropical Africa's most important seed distributors.[9] In tropical Central and South America, toucans and trogons provide this vital service.[10]

On plains and other open areas, vultures provide natural sanitation services by scavenging animal carcasses.[11] Hummingbirds, orioles, and other nectar-feeding birds pollinate a wide variety of wildflowers, shrubs, and trees, including many valued by people. Meanwhile, thousands of insect-eating species and hundreds of rodent- and insect-eating raptors keep pests in check.[12] In Canadian forests, for instance, populations of wood warblers and evening grosbeaks surge to match outbreaks of spruce budworms, insects that can severely damage forests of spruce and fir.[13] The loss of these birds and their vital ecological contributions tugs at the interconnected fabric of ecosystems.

In addition, many bird species are easily seen or heard, making them excellent environmental indicators. In many cases, they provide scientists with the best glimpse at how humanity's actions affect the world's ecosystems and wildlife.[14] In Europe, biologists consider dippers, round-bodied stream-living songbirds, valuable indicators of clean water because they feed on sensitive bottom-dwelling insects such as caddisfly larvae, which disappear in sullied waters. The disappearance of dippers and their prey also follows water acidification brought on by acid rain or the replacement of native deciduous forests with pine plantations. Other species are important indicators of varied threats to humanity, including chemical contamination, disease, and global warming.[15]

Ornithologists are compiling status reports for all of the world's species, but what they already know is alarming.[16] (See Box 1, page 12.[17]) Human-related factors threaten 99 percent of the species in greatest danger. Bird extinctions are on the increase. At least 128 species have vanished over the last 500 years; of these, 103 have become extinct since 1800 and several dozen since 1900.[18] On islands, human-caused bird extinctions are not new: scientists recently concluded that even before European explorers sailed into the region, human colonization of Pacific islands wiped out up to 2,000 bird species that were endemic (found nowhere else). Today, however, peo-

BOX 1

Regional Estimates of Bird Declines

There is no single comprehensive worldwide survey of bird declines, but a broad global picture can be assembled from recent regional surveys, even though they employ varying methodologies:

• A 1994 study revealed that 195 of 514 European bird species (38 percent) had "unfavorable conservation status."

• In 2002, 65 percent of 247 species found in the United Kingdom fell under some category of conservation concern, rating as either "red" or "amber" status. Only 35 percent fell under the "green," or steady and stable, category.

• Based on the North American Breeding Bird Survey's records between 1966 and 1998, some 28 percent of 403 thoroughly monitored species showed statistically significant negative trends. In 2002, the National Audubon Society declared that more than a quarter of U.S. birds were declining or in danger.

• A 2001 BirdLife International study of Asian birds found 664 of the region's bird species (one-quarter of the total) in serious decline or limited to small, vulnerable populations.

• Some Australian ornithologists believe that half of their island nation's land bird species, including many endemic parrots, could become extinct by the end of the century, although recent breeding bird surveys chronicled little difference in status for most species over the past 20 years.

Source: See Endnote 17 for this section.

ple are crowding out bird populations on mainlands as well.[19]

Birds are by no means the only class of animals at risk, of course. Many scientists now consider the world to be in the midst of the sixth great wave of animal extinctions. The fifth wave finished off the dinosaurs 65 million years ago.[20] Unlike previous episodes, however, humans are behind most of the current round of sudden die-offs. One-quarter of the world's mammal species are threatened or nearly threatened with extinction; of the other well-surveyed species, 25 percent of reptiles, 21 percent of amphibians, and 30 percent of fish are threatened.[21]

But if we focus solely on the prospects of extinction, we partly miss the point. From an ecological perspective, extinction is only the last stage in a spiraling degeneration that sends a thriving species slipping toward oblivion. Species stop functioning as critical components of their ecosystems well before they completely disappear. And as conservationists are learning from species reintroduction programs, conserving healthy bird populations now proves far simpler than trying to reconstruct them later.[22]

Although birds are probably the best-studied animal class, a great deal remains to be learned about them, from their life histories to their vulnerability to environmental change. In tropical countries where both avian diversity and habitat loss are greatest—such as Colombia, the Democratic Republic of the Congo (formerly Zaire), and Indonesia—experts just do not know the full scope of bird declines because many areas remain unsurveyed. (See Table 2, page 14.[23]) Species, and distinct populations that may later be considered separate species, may vanish even before scientists can classify them or study their behavior, let alone their ecological importance.[24] Every year, several new bird species are described. One of the century's first was an owl discovered in Sri Lanka in January 2001, the first new bird species found there in 132 years.[25] Other species, while known to science, have not been seen in years but may still survive. These scarce birds sit at a crossroads, as does humanity. One path leads toward continued biodiversity and sustainability. The other leads toward extinction and imbalance.

Habitat Loss: The Greatest Threat

During the 20th century, the human population mushroomed from 1.6 billion to over 6 billion. Settlers fanned out along spreading webs of roadway, chiseling settlements into frontier areas. Industries grew, increasing demand for natural resources. Commerce between nations became increasingly international. The rapid changes transformed once-extensive

TABLE 2

The World's Most Bird-Diverse Countries

Country	Number of Bird Species	Diversity Ranking by Other Taxa		
		Mammals	Reptiles	Amphibians
Colombia	1,815	4	3	1
Peru	1,703	9	12	7
Brazil	1,622	1	5	2
Ecuador	1,559	13	8	3
Indonesia	1,531	2	4	6
Venezuela	1,360	10	13	9
India	1,258	8	6	8
China	1,244	3	7	5
Dem. Rep. of Congo	1,094	7	14	16
Mexico	1,050	5	2	4

Note: Countries in boldface type rank among the top 10 countries with the most threatened bird species.

Source: See Endnote 23 for the Introduction.

wilderness into precarious habitat islands.[1] Today, loss or damage to species' living spaces poses by far the greatest threat to birds and biodiversity in general.[2]

These days, looking at a map of the world's biomes (major climate-influenced ecological communities, such as deserts and tropical rainforests) gives more a picture of how things were a few centuries ago than how they are now. Timber operations, farms, pastures, and settlements have already claimed almost half of the world's forests. Between the 1960s and 1990s, about 4.5 million square kilometers of the world's tropical forest cover (20 percent) were cut or burned.[3] Estimates of deforestation rates vary, from 50,000 to 170,000 square kilometers per year.[4] Perhaps easier to track are dwindling populations of creatures that must live beneath the trees: habitat loss jeopardizes 1,008 (85 percent) of the world's most threatened bird species, with recent tropical forest destruction affecting 74 percent of these.[5]

Foresters herald the re-growth of temperate forests as an environmental success story, and in recent decades substantial reforestation has taken place in, for example, the eastern

United States, China, and Europe. Forest management profoundly affects diversity and natural balances, however, and satellite images of tree cover do not tell us how much of the re-grown forest is quality habitat.[6] In the southeastern United States over the last five years, for instance, more than 150 industrial chip mills have chewed up vast tracts of natural forest to produce paper, rayon, and pressboard. Foresters replace the clearcut area with rows of same-age, same-species pine saplings. For many native animals and plants, simplified plantation monocultures are no substitute for more complex natural forests, with their mix of old, young, living, dead, deciduous, and coniferous trees, and lush, varied undergrowth.[7] Even without plantations, the consistent loss of some forest components can cause birds to abandon areas. For example, studies in intensively managed Finnish forests, where foresters remove older and dead trees, revealed marked declines in large forest birds such as a peacock-sized grouse called the capercaillie and the crow-sized black woodpecker.[8]

To perpetuate the full spectrum of bird species, conservationists need to preserve a full spectrum of habitats, including transitional stages of plant succession. Losses of these areas have been less publicized, but no less dramatic, than the loss of mature forests. North America's eastern towhees, brown thrashers, yellow-breasted chats, and other thicket songbirds require shrubby growth that springs up after a field is idled. This tangled habitat prevails for less than a decade before forest closes in. Today, many shrubland species are in decline, as abandoned farm fields and other transitional areas are swallowed up by development or are fully reclaimed by forest.[9]

Birds tied to grassland areas face even more difficult futures. In many areas, their survival is tied to fire, which at one time periodically swept across the prairies, weeding out tree saplings and encouraging new grass growth. Centuries of farming, overgrazing, and fire suppression have left few large, undisturbed grassland areas. In North America, for example, less than 4 percent of tallgrass prairie habitat remains.[10]

Following this wholesale landscape change, many North American grassland bird populations are ailing. Since 1977, 16 of the 25 most grassland-dependent bird species have declined steadily.[11] The victims include the burrowing owl and other birds that maintain ecological relationships with once-abundant prairie dogs. After these colonial rodents' populations plummeted by 98 percent, the owls, which nest in old prairie dog burrows, disappeared from much of their former breeding range.[12]

In Europe, agriculture claims about half of the land. Most of this area, now under "modern" cultivation, is inhospitable to many birds that adapted over the centuries to pastures, fields of cereals or alfalfa, and other grassland-like habitats. The birds, including harriers, bustards, and larks, declined because intensive modern cultivation often requires herbicides and pesticides that destroy their nesting cover and food base. Also, many crops grown in irrigated areas do not provide ample food or safe cover. Adjacent areas once rich in wildflowers and wild grasses have been plowed under to make way for large machines and larger areas of cropland. Other wildlife-rich components of traditional farms have also declined. Since World War II, for example, more than 120,000 miles of bird-attracting British hedgerows, once grown by small farm owners to separate fields and to fence in livestock, have been ripped out to make way for large, machine-harvested fields and housing developments.[13] The last strongholds for many European grassland birds, including large areas in Portugal, Spain, and central and eastern European countries, are (or soon will be) under severe pressure from increased irrigation and modernization programs subsidized by the European Union's Common Agricultural Policy.[14]

Grassland remains in about 60 percent of its original range in Asia, Africa, and Australia, although much of it is degraded. One widespread threat is overgrazing.[15] In many areas, light grazing helps maintain healthy grasslands. But the picture quickly changes when a threshold, which varies by region, is passed. However, overgrazing is often only one of several threats to these ecosystems.[16] For example, 10 of the world's 25 bustard species are either threatened with extinction or close to it due to widespread overgrazing, collisions with fog- or darkness-shrouded power lines, and hunting.[17]

Wetlands, like forest and grassland habitats, are likewise under assault in ways that gravely threaten birds and myriad other creatures. The pulse of biodiversity quickens where water meets land; there, birds are players in a natural symphony that also embraces crustaceans, fish, amphibians, and much other wildlife. Although people are dazzled by flamingoes, spoonbills, herons, ducks, and other wetland birds, they have traditionally reviled their habitats as mosquito havens or wasted space. During the 20th century, draining, filling, and conversion to farmland or cities destroyed an estimated half of the world's wetlands. Estimates within individual countries are often much higher. Spain, for instance, has lost an estimated 60–70 percent of its wetland area since the 1940s.[18]

Even expansive wetland areas such as Everglades National Park, in the United States, and Spain's Doñana National Park have not been spared humanity's heavy hand. In and around these two greatly compromised protected areas—both of which are classified as Biosphere Reserves, World Heritage Sites, and Ramsar Wetlands of International Importance*—hydrology has been disrupted, exotic plants and animals have invaded, and pesticides and other pollutants wash in from nearby farms and industries.[19] Declinines in bird populations have followed habitat degradation in both parks.[20]

Outside protected areas, changes have been far more dramatic. Over the last 70 years, Armenia's Lake Sevan suffered dramatic lowering due to water diversion, and Lake Gilli was drained entirely. With their vital wetlands destroyed, at least 31 locally breeding bird species abandoned the lakes, including the sensitive black stork and the more adaptable lesser black-backed gull.[21]

A 1999 survey of 47 wetland sites in Morocco found that only 10 had protected status and that most faced threats from development, habitat alteration, and exotic fish introductions. Researchers compared descriptions from a similar sur-

---

* Wetlands that are singled out because of their ecological importance for inclusion in the intergovernmental Ramsar Convention on Wetlands, signed in Ramsar, Iran, in 1971. Designated wetlands are meant to be protected, monitored, and sustainably managed.

vey of 24 of these sites in 1978 and found that 25 percent of the wetlands were destroyed in two decades.[22] Morocco's wetlands are vital for such threatened species as marbled duck and the critically endangered slender-billed curlew.[23]

Aside from being vital nesting grounds for birds, wetlands also serve as key stopover sites for millions of transcontinental migrants, particularly on coasts, along rivers, or in bays where birds pause to rest and refuel before or after transoceanic journeys. Major examples of these rest spots include China's Deep Bay, Suriname's coastal mudflats, Alaska's Copper River Delta, and Australia's Gulf of Carpentaria.[24]

Other concentration points favored by migrating storks, hawks, and songbirds include narrow land corridors such as those at Gibraltar, Turkey's Bosporus Strait, Eilat in Israel, Point Pelee in Canada, and the coastal Mexican city of Veracruz.[25] Previously unknown examples of such vital passageways are still being found. In 1999, U.S. and Costa Rican ornithologists confirmed local reports of seasonal raptor concentrations in Costa Rica's Talamanca region. Ornithologists and bird-watchers later counted almost 3 million raptors passing through the corridor while migrating between North and South America.[26]

Migratory birds naturally face many perils, among them storms, predators, and food shortages. Habitat loss heightens these dangers and presents new ones. At many top migration sites, development shrinks wetlands and other habitats and thereby stresses bird populations.[27] Consider, for example, the American redstart. A recent study of the redstart used carbon isotopes to determine wintering habitats of birds migrating to New Hampshire to breed. The findings suggest that earlier-arriving, healthier birds winter in humid tropical forests, while weaker, less competitive individuals settle for degraded, drier habitats. This likely indicates that optimal redstart wintering areas are already saturated and limited, and implies that although birds can winter in compromised habitats, doing so leaves them less fit to compete and breed.[28] Another study hypothesized that Wilson's warblers, particularly inexperienced young birds, seem to be vulnerable to habitat alteration and marginally productive stopover habitats such as farm fields, especially in fall during the birds' first southward migrations.[29]

In many cases, neotropical migratory birds' winter ranges are more compact than their nesting areas, putting concentrated wintering populations at greater risk from habitat loss. For instance, the scissor-tailed flycatcher (the Oklahoma state bird) nests throughout that state, in most of Texas and Kansas, and in portions of Arkansas, Missouri, and Louisiana. During the winter, however, most of the population packs into an area of northwestern Costa Rica about the size of one Texas county.[30]

Quite a different situation exists for many tropical birds that do not migrate, many of which live year-round in small areas. All told, 2,561 bird species (over one-quarter of all known bird species) occur only within (are endemic to) ranges no larger than 50,000 square kilometers—about the size of Costa Rica or Denmark. (See Figure 1, page 20.) More than half of these species are threatened or near-threatened. Within their limited ranges, many of these localized species are pigeonholed into only those prime habitats that remain. Even in these last havens, other factors often come into play, nudging populations closer to extinction.[31]

Ecologically speaking, what happens around a habitat is as important to its denizens as what happens inside it. In recent years, this revelation began guiding conservationists, who now view protected areas as part of larger landscapes that function together to support or threaten species. When habitats (and mosaics blending different habitats) are diced into smaller and smaller pieces, they often suffer from "edge effect," the negative influences of an edge on a habitat's interior.[32]

For instance, when loggers remove a large swath of trees, light-tolerant plants move into the clearing and the adjacent forest's edge. Sunlight penetrates farther into the forest than before, raising temperatures, drying out the forest floor, and increasing the likelihood of fires or of wind or drought damage. Edge effect stresses or kills shade-adapted plants, leaving them to dry up or to become more susceptible to disease or invading competitors.[33] Researchers studying forest fragments in Brazil's Amazonia region found that the amount of above-ground veg-

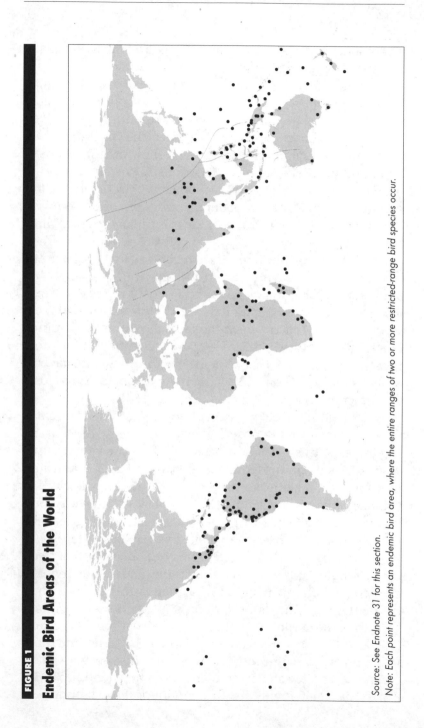

FIGURE 1

Endemic Bird Areas of the World

Source: See Endnote 31 for this section.

Note: Each point represents an endemic bird area, where the entire ranges of two or more restricted-range bird species occur.

etation was greatly reduced, especially within 100 meters of fragment edges, due in good part to increased tree mortality.[34]

After trees fall, remaining forest fragments may no longer provide an ideal habitat for forest interior birds, which must contend with the invasion of creatures that thrive in more open areas. In forest fragments, North American forest birds face larger predator populations as well as brown-headed cowbirds. Rather than building their own nests, cowbirds lay their eggs in nests of host bird species, often to the detriment of the hosts' young. In some highly fragmented forests, cowbird eggs turn up in as many as 90 percent of wood thrush nests and 80 percent of warbling vireo nests.[35]

When isolated in small forest patches, many southeastern Australian birds decline because aggressive, edge-favoring birds called noisy miners out-compete them for food and nesting places. Conservationists now recommend setting aside large forest reserves as one of the few ways to protect smaller, less aggressive species, including many insect-eating birds that live within the miners' breeding range.[36] A similar recommendation has been made for wood thrushes in highly fragmented midwestern U.S. forests. Specialized insectivorous birds also suffer from fragmentation in Japan and other parts of the world.[37]

Roads and power lines frequently cut through forests, fragmenting them, increasing the chance of fatal collisions, and providing pathways for edge predators, competitors, and exotic plants. Traffic noise may also interfere with birds' attempts to mark territory through song. Roads give settlers easier access to forest fragments, where they remove undergrowth and dead standing trees important to parrots, woodpeckers, and other cavity-nesting birds. Intensive hunting often follows when roads cut into forests.[38]

All habitats (not only forests) are vulnerable to the deleterious effects of fragmentation. For example, a recent study of the flightless, ostrich-like greater rhea on Argentina's Pampas grasslands suggests that recent separation of rhea populations due to habitat loss and fragmentation decreased the birds' genetic interchange and diversity.[39] A study of an isolated Illinois population of greater prairie chickens found similar results.[40]

Fragmentation raises the importance of intact "source" areas—refuges producing surplus birds that may later disperse and repopulate more stressed, less productive "sink" areas such as woodlands carved up by suburbs. In a 1996–98 study of an area mostly within Cherokee and Nantahala-Pisgah national forests in the southeastern United States, researchers compared current survey results with surveys of the same sites performed 50 years earlier. They found that this extensive area "retained and probably regained functional integrity for forest birds during the latter half of the 20th century." Nest-robbing blue jays, which thrive in suburbs and other disturbed habitats, declined during this time, while nest-parasitizing cowbirds were virtually absent, probably because there were no open feeding areas nearby. Neotropical migrants declining in many other places held steady or increased in these large forest reserves.[41]

Alien Attacks

With its non-native wild pigs, mongooses, cats, rats, and introduced diseases and bird species, Hawaii provides a dramatic example of how, even in seemingly pristine wildlife habitats, a new order is taking hold. Exotic species have been, and continue to be, introduced intentionally and accidentally. With the rise in global trade and travel over the past century, the pace of introductions has greatly accelerated.[1]

Today, exotics threaten birds and their ecosystems in myriad ways, constituting the second most intense threat to birds worldwide, after habitat loss and degradation. (For threatened species, however, exotics rank third, behind exploitation, particularly hunting and capture for the cage bird trade.)[2]

Once introduced, some exotic predators became all the more lethal on islands, where endemic species evolved with few or no defenses against such hunters. To date, 93 percent of bird extinctions (119 out of 128) recorded since 1500 have

occurred on islands, where extremely vulnerable endemic species succumbed to habitat loss, hunting, and, in most cases, exotic species. Exotic species now menace a quarter of globally threatened bird species.[3]

One reptilian invader, the brown tree snake, ate 12 of Guam's 14 land bird species into extinction by the 1980s after its accidental release following World War II. In recent years, this snake has also turned up at Hawaiian airports, raising fears that it could become the latest—and one of the greatest— threats introduced there.[4]

Introduced rats, often descended from shipboard stow-aways, plague many island birds, including albatrosses and petrels.[5] A recent study of New Zealand's northern offshore islands revealed that rats not only threaten the islands' petrel young and eggs, they also eat native plants' seeds, stifling the distribution of 11 out of 17 coastal trees and pushing some close to local extinction.[6]

Introduced to rid islands of rats, predatory mongooses expanded their diets to include native birds. Intentionally released small Indian mongooses helped bring about the near-extinction or extinction of such endemic birds as the Jamaican pauraque, the Jamaican petrel, the Puerto Rican nightjar, and Semper's warbler on the island of St. Lucia. They pose similar problems in Hawaii and on the Indian Ocean island of Mau-ritius, where sailors and settlers killed off the famed dodo in the 1600s.[7] Meanwhile, introduced Javan mongooses are driv-ing the Okinawa rail, discovered in 1981, toward extinction on its namesake island.[8]

Domestic cats are sofa-loungers and tidbit scroungers in homes worldwide, but felines roaming outside become efficient predators of native wildlife and have a significant effect on bird populations. On many islands, house and feral cats have con-tributed to the extinction of 22 or more endemic birds.[9] They are just as deadly on the mainland: studies in Australia in the early 1990s documented domesticated and feral cats killing members of almost a quarter of the country's 750 bird species.[10] Annually, cats kill an estimated 1 billion birds in the United States, where at least 40 million house cats regularly roam free

and another 60–100 million cats live in a feral state.[11]

Often thought of more as prey than threats, some introduced insects are now turning the table on birds. The yellow crazy ant, a frenetic, fast-multiplying insect, is marching across the Australian territory of Christmas Island following its introduction there during the 1930s. The ants now occupy 2,400 hectares of rain forest, much of it in Christmas Island National Park. Recently, biologists documented the insects killing the islands' endemic terrestrial red crabs. Like many other ant species, crazy ants "farm" scale insects, herding and protecting them and drinking a sweet fluid they secrete while destroying rainforest trees. As of September 2002, Environment Australia and Monash University scientists began dropping poison ant baits via helicopter onto the island's rugged forests.[12]

As they spread across the island, crazy ants will likely kill young native birds, including those of two critically endangered species: the endemic Christmas Island hawk-owl and Abbott's booby, a seabird that nests exclusively in the island's forest canopy. In coming decades, both species are expected to decline 80 percent due to the ant invasion. Introduced crazy ants also threaten birds on the Hawaiian and Seychelles islands and on the Tanzanian island of Zanzibar.[13]

Introduced pathogens and parasites can devastate native bird populations that have yet to develop defenses against them. On the Hawaiian Islands, introduced mosquitoes, which originally landed in the archipelago in ship-carried water barrels in 1826, unleashed the deadly diseases avian pox and avian malaria upon the island's non-immune native birds. These diseases arrived via introduced birds and were injected into natives by the mosquitoes, contributing to at least 10 extinctions. Weakened native Hawaiian birds become even more vulnerable to introduced birds that compete with them for food and habitat.[14]

Endemic birds of Ecuador's Galápagos Islands are struggling with three newly reported parasitic fly species that were most likely recent introductions. The first was identified in 1997. The parasites appear to cause higher chick mortality, and now widely occur in nests and on nestlings on some of the

islands. Among other birds, at least 7 of the 13 endemic Darwin's finches now host the flies, including the endangered mangrove finch, of which only about 110 individuals remain.[15]

Other maladies—whether introduced, naturally occurring, or strengthened by unnatural conditions—also threaten birds. India's populations of the once-abundant long-billed and white-rumped vulture have plummeted more than 90 percent country-wide during the last decade, most likely due to a virus or other contagious illness. A decade ago, these birds swarmed over the abundant cow carcasses that litter fields and dumps around Indian cities and towns. Now they are listed as critically endangered. In their absence, feral dog, crow, and rat populations have surged, taking up the slack in scavengers and posing great health risks to people nearby.[16]

Due to their apparent lack of immunity, North American birds today are key indicators of the spread of West Nile virus, which first appeared in New York in 1999. This mosquito-borne disease, present in Africa and Eurasia for decades, has killed scores of people in the United States so far. West Nile virus has taken a far higher toll on birds, killing thousands of more than 100 species and putting endangered-species breeding programs in peril.[17]

Predators and pathogens aside, native birds also face both genetic and direct competition from other birds that have been introduced or escaped from aviaries. In Spain, for instance, threatened white-headed ducks, already pinched by habitat loss, now mingle and hybridize with North American ruddy ducks. Ruddy ducks found their way to Spain from England after their introduction there in the 1940s.[18] New European legislation aims to curb ruddy duck numbers through hunting.[19]

Introduced plants create their own, very different dangers, changing bird habitats until they are eventually uninhabitable. Whether brought over as nursery stock, planted with the blessing of farm programs, or seeded by accident, exotic plant species have gone wild in many parts of the world—at the expense of birds and other wildlife. One of North America's worst plant invaders illustrates the point. Brought over from Eurasia, rapid-growing cheatgrass has spread far and wide

since its introduction to North America in the late 1800s.[20] As it overtakes sagebrush and bunchgrass habitats, cheatgrass fuels the decline of such sage-dependent birds as the sage grouse, which nests among sagebrush shrubs and depends on their leaves and shoots for food.[21] Cheatgrass is now found on about 40 million hectares, an area larger than Germany.[22]

Unknowingly, birds use their formidable seed-distributing abilities to further spread invasive exotic plants. This is happening, for example, on Tahiti and in the Hawaiian Islands, where birds distribute seeds of the fast-spreading miconia tree. This South American ornamental now shades out native plant life in more than half of Tahiti's forests.[23] Many scientists consider the striated, broad-leafed plant to be one of the greatest threats to Hawaii's remaining native forests as well; there it covers about 4,400 hectares.[24]

Dealing with exotic introductions often requires active management, including hunting, poisoning, herbicide spraying, and in some cases introducing natural predators of the out-of-control exotic—activities that can also potentially disturb or harm native birds and other wildlife.[25] In the United States alone, estimates of the annual cost of damage caused by exotics and the measures to control them reach as high as $137 billion.[26]

Exploitation:
Hunting, Capture, and Fishing

It is hard not to marvel at tiny birds' awe-inspiring migratory abilities and delight in their return each year. In some regions, however, human attention to migrants poses an environmental problem: unregulated or poorly regulated hunting along migration routes. The Mediterranean island nation of Malta has long had one of the most publicized problems. There, throughout spring and fall migration, hunters take aim at island-hopping birds during their flights north to mainland European nesting grounds and south to African wintering areas.[1] The nongovernmental organization (NGO) BirdLife Malta estimates

that three million birds are shot or trapped in Malta each year.[2]

Meanwhile, illegal or poorly regulated hunting and trapping of protected birds of prey and songbirds remain problems in other parts of Europe, including Cyprus (another important migration stopover), Greece, France, Spain, and Italy, although growing public support for conservation efforts has helped reduce this threat, particularly in the latter two countries.[3] On the other side of Eurasia, an upswing in commercial hunting of Chinese songbirds raises concerns that migratory and resident species, including yellow-breasted buntings and Eurasian tree sparrows, are being unsustainably killed for bite-sized snacks. Despite a government ban, since the early 1990s more than 100,000 a year have been caught, killed, frozen, and then fried and sold, from Beijing to Guandong.[4]

While many small species are targeted, robust species attract even more attention. Turkey-like birds called curassows, chachalacas, and guans are among the first animals to disappear when hunters penetrate Central and South American forests. Large, non-migratory, and palatable, these herbivores feed on forest fruits, seeds, leaves, and flowers, and some are important seed dispersers. Fifteen are now threatened with extinction.[5] Elsewhere, unregulated hunting threatens other large birds, including 22 localized Asian pheasant species.[6]

Hunting is less of a threat for parrots, long loved by people the world over for their colorful plumage, potential affection toward their owners, and, in many species, adept "talking" abilities. For these attributes, wild parrot populations suffer greatly from the wild bird trade. Almost one-third of the world's 330 parrot species is threatened with extinction due to habitat loss and collecting pressures.[7]

Over the last decade, protection measures have helped reduce the international trade in wild parrots. These initiatives include the Convention on International Trade in Endangered Species of Wild Fauna and Flora (CITES), which protects rare species from the wildlife trade (see Box 2, page 28[8]), and wild bird export bans in Australia, Ecuador, Guyana, and other countries. The 1992 Wild Bird Conservation Act in the United States, which limits or prohibits exotic wild bird imports,

BOX 2

Some International Agreements That Help Conserve Birds

Ramsar Convention on Wetlands (1971)
Nearly 1,200 wetland sites in 133 countries, totaling 103 million hectares, have been designated for protection and monitoring under this international agreement to conserve wetlands and use them sustainably.

Programme on Man and the Biosphere (1972) **and**
World Heritage Convention (1972)
Under UNESCO, these initiatives set a framework for designating, protecting, and monitoring some of the world's most important biodiversity and cultural hotspots. As of May 2002, 94 countries had established a total of 408 biosphere reserves under the Man and the Biosphere Programme.

Convention on International Trade in Endangered Species of Wild Fauna and Flora (1975)
An international agreement by 160 countries to monitor international trade in wild animals and plants and ensure that trade does not put wildlife in jeopardy.

Convention on the Conservation of Migratory Species of Wild Animals (1983)
Eighty countries have signed this agreement, also known as the Bonn Convention, to protect migratory wildlife species, including birds, throughout their international migratory, breeding, and wintering areas.

Convention on Biodiversity (1992)
A total of 185 countries have signed on to this agreement, introduced at the Earth Summit in Rio de Janeiro in 1992. Signatories promise to set up strategies for protecting their biodiversity, including habitat protection and restoration. Fewer than 40 have drawn up formal plans so far.

Source: See Endnote 8 for this section.

greatly reduced the influx of wild-caught birds into the country and has boosted a growing U.S. captive-breeding industry.[9]

But protection laws in many parrot-rich countries often go unheeded or do not acknowledge intense domestic demand (e.g., Ecuador), while parrot poaching and smuggling remain widespread due to both domestic and international demand.[10] According to TRAFFIC, an international NGO dedicated to ensuring proper CITES implementation, illegal parrot smuggling remains a significant part of the world's multi-billion-dollar annual trade in wildlife.[11]

In addition to parrots, bird traders seek many other colorful species, including South America's yellow cardinal and a cherry-red bird called the red siskin, both of which have been collected almost to extinction in their remaining habitats. Without concerted in-country efforts to stem unbridled collecting, these and other species will likely disappear.[12]

Direct exploitation aside, birds fall prey to the wasteful secondary effects of another form of wildlife exploitation, commercial longline fishing. At least 23 seabird species now face extinction largely because of this industry, which became dominant worldwide following the 1993 ban on vast drift-nets that scooped up enormous numbers of untargeted sea creatures. Today, longline boats set lines up to 130 kilometers long and studded with as many as 12,000 baited hooks, later hauling them in to collect commercial fish such as tuna, swordfish, cod, and halibut. Hundreds of thousands of seabirds, including albatrosses and petrels, drop down on the lines before they sink, grabbing at bait and becoming hooked, only to be submerged and drowned.[13] To date, no adjustments have been made in fishing practices, despite recent findings that simple measures can reduce bird bycatch by more than 90 percent. Such measures include installing bird-scaring streamers, setting nets at night, and adding weights to lines so that they sink faster.[14] At least 33 countries have longline fleets plying the world's waters; prominent players include the United States, Japan, China, Taiwan, South Korea, Russia, and Canada.[15]

This situation may soon improve. In 2001, seven countries—Australia (which initiated the plan in 1997), Brazil, Chile, France, New Zealand, Peru, and the United Kingdom—signed the Agreement for the Conservation of Albatrosses and Petrels, under the Bonn Convention to protect migratory species. When ratified, this agreement will legally bind signatories to reduce longlining bycatch of seabirds and to implement other seabird conservation measures. One challenge will be to get boats to use these measures uniformly. Then there is the problem of regulating and policing illegal fishing, which

depletes not only bird but also fish stocks. The UN Food and
Agriculture Organization also encourages countries to draw up
their own national plans of action for voluntarily reducing
longlining bird kills.[16]

Chemical Threats

The specter of oil spills also hangs over many seabird populations. An unprecedented volume of oil crosses the seas
these days, providing a human-transported disaster waiting to
happen any time. African, Magellanic, Galápagos, and five other
penguin species are among the many seabirds affected by oil
spills in or near their nesting and feeding areas.[1]

Large-scale spills highlight oil's effects on ecosystems
and birds. The 1989 *Exxon Valdez* spill—at 11 million gallons
the largest U.S. oil spill—probably killed more than 250,000
birds.[2] A 1999 spill off of France's Brittany Coast killed an estimated 100,000–200,000 birds of at least 40 different species.[3]
Between 1990 and 2002, South Africa alone had 10 major oil
spills along its bird-rich coastline, including the 2002 spill from
the Italian ship *Jolly Rubino* on the edge of the St. Lucia Wetlands Reserve, a World Heritage site. But small, less-publi-
cized, daily tanker leaks also kill birds.[4]

In addition to increased traffic, aging tankers and lax reg-
ulations make the business of transporting oil even more
hazardous. This was highlighted in November 2002 when the
tanker *Prestige* broke up off the northwest coast of Spain,
sank, and continued to leak oil from its resting place more than
two miles beneath the surface. A significant portion of the
ship's 77,000-ton cargo of fuel oil slipped into the sea, coat-
ing much of the Galicia region's coastline and fouling beaches
as far east as France. Fishing communities and tourism-
dependent towns were devastated. The disaster's early avian
toll, estimated at tens of thousands of dead seabirds, only hints
at the ecological havoc wrought by the accident, which was
one of Europe's worst oil spills.[5] Spain's endangered breeding

population of common murres may have been among the spill's casualties.[6]

Assessing the *Prestige* and other oil spills' damage to birds and other wildlife is difficult. For example, after a spill, typically only a fraction of all killed birds is found. The *Exxon Valdez* estimate came from extrapolations drawn from 30,000 recovered dead birds, those that didn't drift away, sink out of sight, or get carried off by scavengers. Bird population recovery rates after spills vary depending upon species and local conditions.[7]

Terrestrial habitats also face threats from oil and natural gas exploration, extraction, and transport via pipelines. These activities now occur, for example, in Ecuador and Peru, within the some of world's most bird-rich habitats. There, pipelines and wells fragment habitat, sully rivers with erosion and chemicals, and bring new access roads that invite unplanned settlements.[8]

Oil and natural gas operations are but two industries that affect bird life. Effluents released by factories into surrounding waters also leave telltale marks on bird populations. A study published in 2000 seemed to show that immature tree swallows breeding in the PCB-contaminated Hudson River molt into adult coloration earlier, a possible sign that contaminants disrupt the birds' endocrine systems.[9] In a 1999 study, the same authors described how tree swallows nesting at contaminated Hudson sites built smaller, poorer-quality nests than those constructed by tree swallows living elsewhere in New York state. Previous studies highlighted the importance of nest quality for tree swallow nesting success.[10]

Chemicals also threaten birds far outside heavily industrialized zones. Worldwide, pesticides kill millions of birds on water and on land. One 1992 estimate of bird pesticide exposure on United States farmlands put the annual toll at 67 million bird deaths and 672 million birds exposed.[11] Pesticides can weaken birds (making them more susceptible to predators and other dangers), hamper their reproduction, or kill them. For example, the persistent organochlorine pesticide DDT builds up in predatory birds' tissues and causes widespread nesting failure, as was seen in the United States and Britain during the 1950s and 1960s. Such reproductive failure likely still occurs in African raptors.[12] After U.S. law banned DDT in 1972, the country's peregrine falcon, bald eagle, osprey, and brown pelican populations rebounded.[13] Similar rebounds occurred in Britain with such raptors as sparrowhawks after a ban was initiated there.[14]

In 2001, 120 countries signed a pesticide treaty that included a phase-out of DDT except for limited use in controlling malaria. But DDT has not gone away even where it is now banned: this pesticide persists in soil and water even in places where its use was discontinued 30 years ago.[15]

Although not as persistent, some of the new generation of pesticides, including organophosphates and carbamates, are more toxic to birds.[16] One of the most dramatic recent examples of pesticides' danger to birds comes from the Argentine Pampas, where, in the winter of 1996, an estimated 20,000 Swainson's hawks (about 5 percent of the population) died after feeding on insects in alfalfa and sunflower fields sprayed with the insecticide monocrotophos.[17] These birds, which nest in western North America, fly 6,000–12,000 kilometers south in autumn to feed on field insects during the southern spring and summer. Due to public outcry from NGOs and government agencies in the United States, Canada, and Argentina, a major manufacturer of the organophosphate insecticide, Ciba-Geigy (now Novartis), agreed to phase out its sales in areas where the hawks winter. The Argentinean government also banned its use there.[18]

Many bird-toxic pesticides are used worldwide, including fenthion, a chemical used to target not only mosquitoes but also crop-eating birds such as queleas in eastern Africa.[19] Many non-target birds are killed when this pesticide is sprayed over wetlands or croplands. Although fenthion's use is now severely limited in the United States, the Environmental Protection Agency allowed its use in parts of Florida, prompting a lawsuit from environmental groups arguing that less-toxic pesticides would do the job just as well. Fenthion and other bird-killing pesticides banned from the U.S. market remain widely available in many other countries.[20]

Pesticides also affect birds indirectly, either killing off their prey or destroying vegetation they need for shelter and nesting. British gray partridges, for example, declined after insecticides reduced their chicks' invertebrate prey and herbicides suppressed the wild plants among which they nest and feed.[21] Bustards and other birds living on agricultural lands suffer similar effects when malathion, an insecticide used to control locusts, is sprayed on farmlands where they feed.[22]

Even within many protected wetland areas, thousands of birds die each year from another form of chemical threat: lead poisoning. Carefully regulated hunting is frequently an integrated part of bird conservation efforts. In fact, hunters continue to be instrumental in setting aside vital conservation lands in North America, Europe, and elsewhere. But one traditional hunting tool, lead shot, poses grave threats not only to waterfowl but to raptors and other wildlife. Waterfowl are most at risk because they guzzle down spent shot either instead of the pebbles they seek as grit or by accident when rooting underwater for food. Several weeks after ingesting the shot, the slowly poisoned birds die. Eagles and other scavengers feeding on shot ducks also succumb to lead poisoning.[23]

A growing number of countries, including the United States, Canada, and many in Europe, have banned lead shot for use in waterfowl hunting.[24] But many others have not. The U.S. Fish & Wildlife Service estimates that in 1997 alone, the nationwide ban on lead shot used for waterfowl hunting prevented 1.4 million duck poisoning deaths.[25] In 2001, a partial ban began in Spain, where conservationists estimate that up to 70,000 birds die of lead poisoning each year.[26] Loons and other waterfowl also die from ingesting lead fishing sinkers.[27]

Poison-tainted meat gravely threatens raptors in countries such as Spain, where hunting-ground managers or livestock owners illegally set out poisoned baits to kill off wolves and other predators.[28] In the 1990s, poisoned baits were the leading cause of death of endangered Spanish imperial eagles, killing at least 70. The entire breeding population of this species is about 175 pairs.[29]

Other Hazards of a Humanized World

A s technologies advance and human settlements spread, we tailor the landscape to meet our needs for communication, electricity, modern office space, and other amenities. Some of these changes harm birds, which evolved in far different surroundings.

Power lines strung across open country are a leading cause of mortality among Europe's white storks, threatened great bustards, and raptors. Birds taking off in fog or darkness run into the obscured lines, and others are electrocuted when they land on exposed cables atop poles.[1] Studies conducted in Spain, Norway, and elsewhere indicate that putting markers on wires can cut collisions by half or more. Some companies take this step, but it is not yet a widespread practice in most of the world.[2]

Skyscrapers and television, radio, and cellphone towers kill millions of night-flying migrants each year, especially during cloudy or foggy nights. In the United States alone, communication towers may kill up to 40 million birds annually.[3] The structures' pulsing red lights distract the birds, which use light as one of their migratory cues. Many collide with towers or their guy wires while circling the lights. Depending upon weather conditions, the death tolls can be staggering: During just one cloudy night in January 1998, between 5,000 and 10,000 lapland longspurs—sparrow-like birds that breed on tundra but winter far south on farms in the United States— died after hitting one 420-foot-tall Kansas tower. Between 1957 and 1994, 121,000 birds of 123 species turned up dead beneath one 960-foot television tower in Wisconsin.[4]

These threats increase as tall towers and buildings continue to spread across landscapes. More than 40,000 towers above 200 feet are found in the United States, and this total may double over the next decade due to the proliferation of towers needed for mobile phones and new digital television technology. Height is not the only consideration; location is also important. Towers placed along migration corridors or hilltops increase the risks to birds. Few companies or governments have addressed this growing problem, which requires more study to determine the best measures to minimize the effects of light, towers, guy wires, and tall buildings. Some suggested alternatives include replacing pulsing red lights with white strobe lights that might be less confusing to migrants, and building lower towers that do not require deadly guy wires for support.[5]

Location is also a factor in the placement of wind farms along ridge-tops, along shorelines, and in other ecologically sensitive areas worldwide. Some key migration corridors are now targeted for wind farms, including Appalachian ridgetops followed by large concentrations of migrating songbirds and raptors.[6] Although previous studies on bird mortality from wind turbine collisions indicated low mortality, the recent proliferation of taller and faster turbines highlights the need for further study.[7] Few studies have been done on how high various bird species fly during migration, where to place wind farms to avoid harming migrants, and how best to assess bird mortality around existing wind farms.[8]

To the threats posed by these human-made structures must now be added the dangers of human-caused global warming, which is hastened by many of the same activities that destroy habitat: forest clearing, rampant forest fires, road building, and urban expansion. Scientists estimate that Earth's climate warmed 0.3–0.6 degrees Celsius over the past century, and that temperature change will continue and possibly intensify as carbon dioxide and other heat-trapping gases build up in the atmosphere. Already, ecological changes seem to be under way in ecosystems around the world.[9]

For one thing, temperate fauna and flora seem to be changing their schedules. Over the past few decades, scientists have documented earlier flower blooming, butterfly emergence, and frog calling, as well as earlier bird migration and egg-laying dates in Europe and North America. Many temperate bird species' ranges are creeping northward. While this might sound exciting to bird-watchers, it is unclear whether some earlier migrations and northward range extensions match rapid habitat changes. It is unlikely that all natural components will shift simultaneously, adjusting quickly to rapid climate change. Many probably will not.[10]

While some migratory species now arrive back at their nesting grounds earlier, others that adhere to traditional schedules seem to be at a disadvantage. Each spring, insect-eating pied flycatchers migrate north from African wintering areas, arriving at Netherlands nesting grounds at around the same date. However, insect abundance, probably thanks to warmer climate, now peaks earlier, so the birds raise their young out of step with peak food availability.[11]

Climate models and predictions create other disturbing scenarios. Key coastal wetland areas, such as many in Florida, could be inundated as polar ice melts and sea levels rise.[12] Vegetation and climate models exploring moderate climate change scenarios predict that globally threatened spoon-billed sandpipers and red-breasted geese may lose 60 and almost 70 percent, respectively, of their remaining nesting habitat as tundra turns to forest.[13] The warblers and other songbirds that control spruce budworm and other forest pest outbreaks could diminish, worsening the pests' potential for damage. Habitats may change too quickly for many species to adapt.[14]

Global climate change will also likely increase the frequency and severity of weather anomalies that pound bird populations. El Niño events, when ocean temperatures rise and fish stocks fall near many important seabird breeding islands, could finish off rare, localized, and declining species such as the Galápagos penguin, which has evolved and thrived on an equatorial archipelago bathed by cool, fish-rich currents.[15] In addition, intensified and more-frequent droughts and fires could accompany El Niño and other cycles, both in the tropics and as far north as Canada's boreal forests.[16]

With climate change upon us, conservationists and planners must now think of landscapes and protections as more dynamic than previously supposed. Barriers created by human landscape changes will likely stifle species' movements, and conservation plans will have to take such dangers into account and be flexible enough to accommodate distribution shifts by establishing wildlife corridors and other measures.[17]

Putting Back the Pieces... and Nature's Response

Though their critics often doubt it, conservationists like to be optimistic. The reality is that birds of many species are far less plentiful than they once were. Some are gone forever, while others live on only in captivity. But some efforts by governments and private organizations to reintroduce bird species paint a bright future for jeopardized species, making the effort worth the time and expense. A few noteworthy examples include:

• The rebound of a black-and-white island songbird called the Seychelles magpie-robin, which is gaining ground after being reintroduced to predator-free islands and after reductions in pesticide use in its habitat.[1]

• In 1999, the peregrine falcon was lifted from the U.S. Endangered Species list following the ban on DDT in the 1970s and decades of protection, captive breeding, and reintroduction programs.[2] The bald eagle may soon follow.[3]

• Other reintroduction programs have brought back pink pigeons to Mauritius, Guam rails to Guam and nearby snake-free Rota, and a flightless parrot called the kakapo to New Zealand.

These efforts to protect endangered species in fragile habitats often secondarily benefit the wildlife sharing these birds' habitats.

However, despite conservationists' best intentions, careful wildlife management can go awry. Even if released or protected animals can re-acclimate to the wild, the wild into which they are released may not be the same. In essence, birds and other wildlife sometimes return to an altered world.

A North American example illustrates how wildlife management efforts can backfire, with adverse ecological consequences. The white-tailed deer, a species over-hunted and scarce at the beginning of the 20th century, now destroys its own habitat to the detriment of many birds and other wildlife. Bolstered by decades of conservation efforts, the North American white-tailed deer population today stands at about 33 million and is growing.[4]

But the forests are not the same: For one thing, the deer's chief natural predators, wolves and mountain lions, were killed off and (mostly) not reintroduced. Today, many deer live in isolated forest fragments where the confined animals degrade their habitat. Studies in the eastern United States chronicle how hungry deer wipe out emerging tree saplings, shrubs, and wildflowers such as lilies, changing forest plant composition and bird life.[5] Woodlands then change in appearance from dense and lush to manicured, i.e., virtually free of under-brush. Without cover, ovenbirds, towhees, woodcocks, and other shrub- and ground-nesting birds decline.[6] Exotic plants such as the Japanese stilt grass thrive in disturbed, deer-grazed soil, over-running struggling native plants.[7]

Like wildlife management efforts, habitat restoration can be surprisingly complicated. How can we re-create habitat when tree or shrub species have vanished, soil is compacted, water tables have dropped, or chemicals have poisoned the area? Costly projects may yield at best marginal results, not fully compensating wildlife for habitats lost. Others may attract long-lost species.

In an effort to re-convert abandoned farms to diverse wet-land, state and federal conservationists established Lake Apopka Restoration Area northwest of Orlando, Florida. The restora-tion program began a century after farms usurped lakeside wet-lands and after algal blooms depleted the lake's aquatic life. In the late 1990s, the St. Johns River Water Management District, helped by federal funds, purchased several farms, and land man-agers flooded the area to control weeds and begin the marsh restoration process. Birds of more than 170 species flocked to the newly created shallow waters, part of a restoration expected to take 25 to 50 years to complete. Branded one of North America's most bird-rich inland habitats, the regenerating Apopka wetlands were registered as an important bird area (IBA).* An estimated 40,000 birds visited on a single day in December 1998.[8]

However, between November 1998 and March 1999, 400

---

* Important bird areas are critical breeding and/or migration spots identified by the NGO BirdLife International.

American White Pelicans were found dead there, along with 90 dead birds of 12 other species. Another 500 white pelicans, likely wanderers from the Lake Apopka farm fields, were found dead in other parts of the state. Investigation by the U.S. Fish & Wildlife Service determined that the fish-eating birds had been poisoned by organochlorine pesticides, such as toxaphene, dieldrin, and DDT derivatives, chemicals used on the old farm fields for decades.[9]

In 1999, managers drained the fields. In 2002, one 700-acre test site was re-flooded with no apparent adverse effects on visiting birds. Other acres with minimally detected residues will be gradually re-flooded, while sites with higher concentrations will have to be cleaned up. Researchers have embarked upon a two-year bio-accumulation study in hopes of better understanding how pesticides pass from sediments to fish to birds.[10]

Taking Stock

Birds are already one of the most studied and best understood animal groups, yet we are still far from a comprehensive understanding of their natural history and ecological needs and contributions around the world. To determine the need for (and focus of) conservation efforts more fieldwork is needed, to varying degrees, in most parts of the world. For example, thorough study is still required to understand the distribution of declining bird species in eastern Europe, and there are still gaps in our knowledge of European and North American birds' feeding, breeding, and migratory habits. (Aleutian terns, for instance, winter in Alaska, but no one has pinpointed their Pacific wintering range nor the route they follow to get there.) Meanwhile, gaping holes remain in our knowledge of many bird species in Africa, Asia, and the Neotropics, or New World tropics.[1]

Bird species' status and distribution can swing quickly or change steadily over time. Watching such trends and determining possible causes is critical for conservation planning. In

1996, biologists Michael A. Patten and Curtis A. Marantz touched on this issue after studying a sudden influx into California of seven species of southeast U.S.-nesting wood warblers and vireos. They wrote, "Some bird species show remarkable plasticity in their breeding ranges.... We feel that: (1) the southeastern species are expanding westward; and/or (2) their populations are increasing, thus increasing the source pool for vagrants to California." In the end, they added: "Only a long-term analysis, with a few more decades of data, can be used to test this hypothesis."[2]

However, birds in many other parts of the world do not have that much time. If they are not located and their conservation needs assessed, they will disappear with their remaining habitat. Fortunately, conservationists have been busy cataloguing key areas for birds. Decades of field work, computer modeling, and satellite imagery analysis have pinpointed "hotspots," areas that harbor disproportionately high diversity and high numbers of imperiled bird species. BirdLife International has been instrumental in working with organizations, agencies, and biologists around the world, creating a global partnership that coordinates conservation efforts. Increasingly, the efforts of this NGO and many others have focused not only on shaping government action but also on working with other NGOs and involving local communities in protecting and learning about endemic birds and other wildlife.[3]

Among BirdLife's most significant accomplishments in this area has been the identification of 7,000 IBAs[4] in 140 countries and 218 endemic bird areas (EBAs), which are places with the highest numbers of restricted-range and endemic species. (See Figure 1, page 20.) While not conferring formal protection, these designations offer a framework on which to base international, national, and local protection priorities. Some IBAs and EBAs are already designated protected areas, and some have active programs to involve local people in protecting the areas. Many, however, remain unprotected and poorly surveyed.[5]

Enter the bird-watcher, or birder, a person who may not be a professional ornithologist but whose intense avocational interest in birds has turned her or him into a supporter of conservation efforts. Growing ranks of birders provide a powerful infusion of eyes and ears that assist scientists in monitoring bird populations in IBAs and other areas important to birds around the world. For example, more than 50,000 volunteers participated in the 100th annual National Audubon Society Christmas Bird Count, the largest and probably longest-running bird census. These knowledgeable amateurs identified and tallied the numbers of birds found wintering at more than 1,800 local census sites throughout North America and in an increasing number of Central and South American, Pacific island, and Caribbean countries. The century's worth of wintering bird data gives ornithologists a telling picture of bird abundance and distribution.[6]

Each year since 1987, birders have conducted similar January surveys across Asia, as teams of local volunteer birders pool their observations in the Asian Waterbird Census. And during the spring nesting season, other large-scale monitoring efforts take place in North America, Europe, Australia, Japan, and elsewhere to canvas bird breeding.[7] Other "citizen science" programs target declining bird species, backyard birds, plants, insects, amphibians, and even stream-living invertebrates (to test stream water quality).[8]

In Australia, more than 700 volunteer bird-watchers teamed up with state and federal biologists to survey the migratory and endangered swift parrot. From 1995 to 2002, this joint effort helped detail the feeding and habitat preferences of this widely dispersing species. Assembling hundreds of biologists to conduct this survey would have been costly if not impossible. The project's data helped win strengthened protective legislation and habitat management for this rare bird.[9]

Conservation Strategies and Priorities

Linking IBAs and other key habitats and striking a balance between developed and undeveloped areas will be key in saving birds in our ever-more-crowded world. Over the past 20 years, the emergence of the multidisciplinary field of conservation biology—a blending of biology, conservation science, economics, and the mutual engagement of conservationists, communities, and businesses—has changed the focus of biodiversity protection efforts from the park to the landscape level. In their plans, conservation biologists not only factor in protected areas but also adjacent lands and water resources as well as the people who inhabit and use them. This landscape focus increasingly positions conservation goals alongside, instead of in confrontation with, business plans.[1]

Until recently, the landscape approach was ignored in favor of snatching and holding prized parkland. Under this approach, wildlife protection was considered something done mostly within designated protected areas. Now, fixed boundaries are showing their imperfections due both to faults in past planning and the pervasive effects of development just outside park borders.

Many park protection efforts from the late 1800s to the mid-1900s focused more on securing beautiful vistas and rock formations than biodiversity. Today, for example, a disproportionately large number of U.S. national parks protect high, rocky mountainous areas and desert compared with more biologically diverse lowland habitats such as wetlands, prairies, and riverside woodlands (although this is not the case with national wildlife refuges).[2]

Even near reserves, the most productive habitats often lie in private hands or at vulnerable park boundaries. Using bird diversity as an indicator, a 2002 study found that, in Greater Yellowstone Ecosystem in Montana and Wyoming, only about 7 percent of bird hotspots fell well within reserve boundaries. Most were at lowland sites vulnerable to development or edge effect.[3]

And even well within their boundaries, large parks face alteration. In general, because they are in some of the world's poorest areas, the largest and most biologically diverse parks, including Peru's Manu National Park—where up to 1,000 species, about 10 percent of the world's bird species, have been recorded—are the least well staffed and protected.[4]

All told, between 6.4 and 8.8 percent of Earth's land area

falls under some category of formal habitat protection. These areas are sprinkled across the globe, and many are quite small. Their management varies from protection only on paper to a mixed strategy that includes core areas closed to visitors and surrounded by buffers that allow recreational and commercial activities.[5]

These park protection measures aside, most of the world remains open to alteration. Conservationists now consider private lands to be great untapped frontiers for wildlife conservation. Many new projects, for example, incorporate conservation easements, legal agreements under which private land owners agree to limit land use activities on their properties in order to protect birds and habitat. Easements are becoming stronger conservation tools in many countries, such as Mexico and the United States, where by 2000 about 12,000 easements protected around three million acres.[6]

Whether on private, unclaimed, or public lands, conservation initiatives require strong local support for sustained success. People who are hungry and lack economic alternatives cannot be expected to embrace efforts to protect natural resources unless they clearly benefit in the bargain. Boosting economic prospects and educational opportunities—that is, empowering communities to rise above poverty—will allow local people to focus on saving birds and other natural resources for the future. These conditions are still lacking in many parts of the world, but an increasing number of efforts highlights the potential for conservation and poverty-fighting measures to work in tandem.[7]

The growing awareness that biodiversity protections can be combined with money-making ventures seems to be bringing enterprise and environmentalism together. Nowhere are marriages between commercial and conservation interests more apparent than in agriculture, the main employer and source of income in many developing nations.[8]

Shade-grown coffee is holding ground, for instance. This crop is grown the traditional way, beneath a tropical forest canopy that also shelters resident and migratory birds. Shade-grown coffee requires far fewer chemical inputs than coffee grown on pesticide-heavy "sun coffee" farms. Some large coffee shop chains now sell these specialty varieties, but the largest brand-name companies have yet to dabble in more environment- and bird-friendly coffees. While acreage in shade-grown coffee may not be growing, conservationists hope to keep remaining acreage from converting to other crops or sun coffee.[9]

In addition, cultivation of various fruits, cork, cacao (for cocoa), and other crops supports many bird species, although they do not fully substitute for natural forests. Farm operations that minimize use of harmful pesticides, such as organic farms and those using integrated pest management, provide more diverse food sources and safer habitats for birds.[10]

Some successful incentive programs pay farmers to set aside land for wildlife, water, and soil conservation. From 2002 to 2007, for example, 15.9 million hectares (39.2 million acres) will be enrolled in the U.S. Department of Agriculture's Conservation Reserve Program (CRP).[11] Hundreds of thousands of farmers enroll land for 10 to 15 years, taking it out of production, planting grasses and trees, restoring wetlands, grazing, or harvesting hay in a way compatible with wildlife and erosion control. Although some grasses used in this program are invasive exotics, since its inception in 1985 the CRP has helped many declining grassland birds regain ground, including sharp-tailed grouse, dickcissels, and Henslow's sparrows.[12]

In the Netherlands, a program set up by Dutch biologists pays dairy farmers to protect and encourage nesting birds as a farm product. An experiment conducted between 1993 and 1996 found that it was cheaper to pay farmers to monitor and manage breeding wild birds as if they were a crop than to compensate them for restricting farming practices to protect birds. The project resulted in increased breeding success of meadow-nesting lapwings, godwits, ruffs, and redshanks, without disrupting the dairy business.[13] By 2002, about 36,000 hectares (89,000 acres) of Dutch farmland were enrolled in this program.[14]

Ecotourism, which first arose in Kenya in the 1960s and Costa Rica in the 1980s, is loosely defined as nature-oriented travel that does not harm the environment and that benefits both the traveler and the local community being visited. Most nations now court ecotourists. Although nature-oriented tourism is not always easy on the environment, this industry shows signs of improving and is often an economically viable alternative to resource extraction.[15]

Some promising programs are under way that involve local communities. One such case is taking shape in South Africa, focused on a village and its endangered blue swallows. As the glossy, streamer-tailed birds sweep over moist, montane grasslands in search of insects, the benefits of their conservation are obvious to community members and visiting ecotourists alike. Recently, BirdLife South Africa and the Endangered Species Trust Blue Swallow Working Group initiated a development program for local blue swallow guides. In 2001, its first guide, Edward Themba, began work in the Blue Swallow Natural Heritage Site, an IBA in the village of Kaapsehoop near Kruger National Park.[16] Other South African projects are being developed using the blue swallow program as a model, and the founders hope it will spur efforts in other countries as well.[17]

Many North American communities are now banking on ecotourists seeking new and unusual bird sightings along driving routes that string together far-flung towns and prime bird habitats. In Florida, for example, a sign-marked route of some 3,000 kilometers, now under development, will wind its way past most of the state's bird hotspots, including county parks, ranches, state forests, private preserves, an alligator farm or two, and federal lands.[18] Texas pioneered the first such driving route in 1996, including 300 sites where birders may find up to 600 bird species. At least 19 other states and several Canadian provinces have followed suit over the last seven years. Local towns benefit from nature tourists, a point not lost on local chambers of commerce.[19]

The development of birding trails follows decades of rising interest in birding, which is now considered one of the fastest-growing outdoor hobbies in the United States. Volunteer bird-watchers, as mentioned earlier, contribute greatly to studies relating to birds, but the hobby's economic clout and popularity are other factors worth mentioning. Two nationwide surveys underscore this point. The *2001 National Survey of Fishing, Hunting, and Wildlife-Associated Recreation*, by the U.S. Departments of Interior and Commerce, reported that more than 66 million Americans aged 16 or older observed, fed, or photographed wildlife (particularly birds) during the year, spending $38 billion on birdseed, binoculars, field guides, and other equipment and travel needs.[20] Another report, the 2001 *National Survey on Recreation and the Environment*, estimates that at least a third of U.S. residents 16 or older (about 70 million people) go outdoors to watch birds sometime during the year, and that these numbers more than doubled between 1983 and 2001. Surveys conducted in the United Kingdom by the Royal Society for the Protection of Birds yielded similar results.[21]

To balance human activities with nature protection, we must create a sustainable land use strategy that ranks biodiversity protection high among development priorities such as economic growth, housing, infrastructure, sanitation, and municipal water supply. Many international, national, and local laws and agreements exist to protect birds and other wildlife. (See Box 1, page 12.) Yet many remain unenforced. Following through on existing laws and agreements would go a long way toward incorporating the needs of wildlife into a sustainable development framework.

A recent episode of cooperation between companies and biologists shows how this can work. In Spain, both Spanish and EU laws prohibit major construction within protected bird areas without careful study and mitigation. Northeast of Madrid, such measures are being put into practice to protect declining steppe birds where highway work threatens part of an area designated both as an internationally recognized IBA and a ZEPA, or bird protection zone selected by Spain under an EU directive. There, the disturbance-sensitive great bustard is considered an indicator species whose status helps scientists monitor the health of steppe habitats in the area.[22]

The construction is creating two stretches of highway that will link Madrid to nearby Guadalajara and will run through the protected area's southern edge. HENARSA, the contractor, set aside more than 6 million Euros of the projects' 420-million-

Euro budget (roughly $450 million) to mitigate loss of grassland bird habitat, and hired a team of biologists from the government scientific research institute CSIC to direct the money toward these conservation measures. "Development is something that's hard to completely avoid," says team leader and CSIC ornithologist Juan Carlos Alonso, who has studied the area's bustards and other steppe birds for 10 years. Although the team preferred that all of the designated habitat remain untouched, they realized that the road-building would be unavoidable and they accepted the company's contract in hopes of minimizing the damage. "If we didn't want to collaborate with this company, they would do it with another team less qualified than we were to advise them," says Alonso. This type of collaboration is becoming more common as conservation and development interests increasingly run into each other.[23]

Through 2006, the team will implement mitigation measures that include expanding cultivation of the bustards' winter food plants such as vetch and alfalfa, paying farmers to leave harvested fields in stubble through the winter to provide food for the birds, studying and marking power lines through key areas (or diverting them) to reduce collision mortality, running public education campaigns to promote support and better understanding of bustard conservation efforts in the area, and buying up hunting rights in a few key areas to keep rabbit and partridge hunters from disturbing bustards.[24]

Using identified IBAs as a guide posts, conservationists are hoping that similar cooperation will soon prevail in eastern Europe, where many transportation changes are slated, particularly in EU expansion countries. Many bird species now rare or extinct in western Europe still thrive to the east, where slower economies delayed development and allowed large areas of wildlife habitat to remain intact. As plans are laid to develop road, rail, and waterway transportation networks in the region's EU expansion nations, environmental groups are asking planners to divert these projects from 85 IBAs that would be threatened along various routes. With areas of top avian diversity already targeted, they hope to prevent destruction of the most important sites.[25]

Birds also live on properties already owned by large companies. And they are not always unwelcome there. While large companies, government agencies, and environmental groups often remain at odds over pollution, habitat destruction, and other issues, a spirit of cooperation is emerging with regards to conservation. Many large, land-holding companies are now getting in on the conservation act, realizing that bird and other wildlife protection improves community relations, polishes environment-friendly images, and makes good use of otherwise idle buffer lands.[26] For instance, a U.S.-based NGO called the Wildlife Habitat Council, founded in 1988 by several major corporations and environmental groups,* partners with companies to set up on-site conservation programs. Such partnerships, as of 2002, affected two million acres at 800 sites owned by 119 companies in most U.S. states, Puerto Rico, and 19 other countries.[27]

Bird and biodiversity conservation is piggy-backed on lands controlled by another large landholder, the U.S. military. For decades, U.S. military installations have preserved large land holdings used as buffer zones, artillery ranges, military exercise areas, airfields, and other installations. Many of the Department of Defense's 25 million acres remain home to species now displaced elsewhere by sprawl, including threatened black-capped vireos and golden-cheeked warblers in Texas, red-cockaded woodpeckers in the southeastern United States, and the palila, a songbird endemic to the Hawaiian Islands. The U.S. military employs wildlife biologists, spends millions to protect endangered species on its properties (more than $38 million in 2000), and works with NGOs to ensure the stability of its on-site conservation programs.[28] Conservation efforts at other military properties around the world could similarly provide longterm protection for wildlife decimated in less restricted areas. Examples include the Korean Demilitarized Zone and the Canal Zone in Panama.

---

* Anheuser-Busch Companies, Inc., DuPont, ExxonMobil, General Electric Company, Tenneco Oil Company, the United States Steel Corporation, American Farmland Trust, Izaak Walton League, National Wildlife Federation, and World Wildlife Fund-U.S.

Some large-scale regional initiatives involving governments, citizens, NGOs, and private companies are blending conservation, commercial, and community activities. One evolving initiative is the Mesoamerican Biological Corridor, an ambitious project that began in 1990 as the Paseo Pantera (Path of the Panther) project. This effort, initially spearheaded by the Wildlife Conservation Society, is now endorsed by regional governments and aims to protect an interconnected wildland corridor stretching from Mexico to Colombia, while promoting more sustainable and equitable development throughout Central America and southern Mexico. The project is designed to protect representative habitats that are home to most of the region's biodiversity while supporting sustainable agroforestry, ecotourism, and other low-impact industries in buffer zones and corridors between and around parks and reserves. So far, the project has been supported by Central American environment agencies, the World Bank, the United Nations, the Global Environment Facility, European donors, the U.S. Agency for International Development, and many NGOs. Among the key areas included in the initiative are existing "peace parks" along once-troubled border areas between Nicaragua and Honduras; Costa Rica and Nicaragua; Guatemala, Mexico, and Belize; and Panama and Costa Rica.[29]

The actions needed to ensure a secure future for birds are the very same ones needed to achieve a sustainable human future: preserving and revitalizing ecosystems, cleaning up polluted areas, reducing the use of harmful pesticides and other chemicals, reversing global climate change, stemming population growth, restoring ecological balances, controlling the spread of exotic species, and so on. Wildlife conservation must be worked into and be compatible with rural, suburban, and urban planning efforts that improve the prospects for the world's poor while making our cities and industries safer for all living beings. A major accomplishment down this road would be to follow through with action on such already-signed agreements as the 1992 Convention on Biodiversity.

In the end, it will be combinations of conservation efforts that bear fruit in preserving biodiversity. Some areas will need strict protection, either public or private, while others will be able to host a mix of commercial and conservation efforts. Planners will need to involve wildlife experts in siting new roadways, railroads, power lines, and towers so as to minimize their effects on birds. And conservation will need to remain a high priority through the inevitable periods of economic and political change.

Of birds, Canadian Wildlife Service biologist F.L. Filion wrote, "It is difficult to imagine another resource capable of contributing as fully and as completely to mankind's diverse needs."[30] Birds provide us with food, inspiration, a link to nature, and an alert system for detecting environmental ills. Today, this feathered resource is in great need of human attention. As we work toward a more sustainable future, keeping an eye on the world's 9,800 bird species helps us keep ourselves in check—if we care to heed the warnings. Along the way, birds' colors, songs, and activity will continue to inspire us, reminding us that in protecting the world's biodiversity, we are doing the right thing for flora, fauna, and ourselves.

Notes

Introduction

1. Josep del Hoyo, Andrew Elliott, and Jordi Sargatal, eds., *Handbook of the Birds of the World, Volume 1* (Barcelona: Lynx Edicions, 1992), pp. 436–50.

2. Holger Schulz, ed., *White Storks on the Up?: Proceedings of the International Symposium on the White Stork*, Hamburg, 1996 (Bonn: NABU, 1999), pp. 20–2, 351–65; phone interview and e-mails from Holger Schulz, May 2001.

3. Schulz, op. cit. note 2, all sources.

4. Convention on Biodiversity website at www.iisd.ca/biodiv/cop5 /index.html, viewed December 2000.

5. Alison J. Stattersfield and David R. Capper, eds., *Threatened Birds of the World* (Barcelona: Lynx Edicions, 2000), pp. 2–20.

6. Josep del Hoyo, Andrew Elliott, and Jordi Sargatal, eds., *Handbook of the Birds of the World, Volume 6* (Barcelona: Lynx Edicions, 2001), pp. 100.

7. Josep del Hoyo, Andrew Elliott, and Jordi Sargatal, eds., *Handbook of the Birds of the World, Volume 2* (Barcelona: Lynx Edicions, 1994), p. 239.

8. Hussein Adan Isack, "The Cultural and Economic Importance of Birds Among the Boran People of Northern Kenya," in A.W. Diamond and F.L. Filion, *The Value of Birds* (Cambridge: International Council for Bird Preservation, 1987), pp. 91–5.

9. Kenneth D. Whitney, Mark K. Fogiel, Aaron M. Lamperti, Kimberly M. Holbrook, Donald J. Stauffer, Britta Denise Hardesty, V. Thomas Parker, and Thomas B. Smith, "Seed Dispersal by *Certatogymna* Hornbills in the Dja Reserve, Cameroon," *Journal of Tropical Ecology*, vol. 14 (1998), pp. 351–71.

10. Del Hoyo et al., op. cit. note 6, pp. 91–2.

11. Deborah J. Pain and Michael W. Pienkowski, eds., *Farming and Birds in Europe* (San Diego: Academic Press, 1997), pp. 128–37.

12. Josep del Hoyo, Andrew Elliott, and Jordi Sargatal, eds., *Handbook of the Birds of the World, Volume 5* (Barcelona: Lynx Edicions, 1999), pp. 499 and 523.

13. A.W. Diamond, "A Global View of Cultural and Economic Uses of Birds," and Daniel A. Welsh, "Birds as Indicators of Forest Stand Condition in Boreal Forests of Eastern Canada," in Diamond and Filion, op. cit. note 8, pp. 106 and 261–4.

14. David Peakall and Hugh Boyd, "Birds as Bio-Indicators of Environmental Conditions," in Diamond and Filion, op. cit. note 8, pp. 113–8.

15. S.J. Ormerod and Stephanie J. Tyler, "Dippers and Grey Wagtails as Indicators of Stream Acidity in Upland Wales," in Diamond and Filion, op. cit. note 8, pp. 191–207.

16. E-mail from Alison J. Stattersfield, Global Species Coordinator for BirdLife International, June 2002.

17. Graham M. Tucker and Melanie F. Heath, *Birds in Europe: Their Conservation Status* (Cambridge, U.K.: BirdLife International, 1994), p. 13; R.D. Gregory et al., "The Population Status of Birds in the U.K.," *British Birds*, vol. 95 (2002), pp. 410–50; U.S. Geological Survey, at www.mbr-pwrc.usgs.gov/bbs /trend/guild99.html, viewed May 2001; "Audubon Releases List of America's Most Imperiled Birds," at www.audubon.org/News/Press_/Releases/index.html, viewed November 2002; Mike Crosby, "Asia's Red Data Birds: The Facts," *World Birdwatch*, June 2001, p. 17; "Half of Australia's Land Birds Predicted To Become Extinct by End of 21st Century," at www.nccnsw.org.au/member /cbn/news/media/19990803_HalfALBExt.html, viewed April 2002; survey results from Stephen Garnett, "Atlas of Australian Birds: Winners and Losers," *Wingspan*, December 2001, p. 23.

18. Stattersfield and Capper, op. cit. note 5, p. 2.

19. David W. Steadman, "Human-Caused Extinction of Birds," in Marjorie L. Reaka-Kudla, Don E. Wilson, and Edward O. Wilson, eds., *Biodiversity II: Understanding and Protecting Our Biological Resources* (Washington, D.C.: Joseph Henry Press, 1996), p. 148.

20. Edward O. Wilson, *The Diversity of Life* (Cambridge, Massachusetts: The Belknap Press of Harvard University Press, 1992), pp. 29–32.

21. C. Hilton-Taylor (compiler), *2002 IUCN Red List of Threatened Species* (Gland, Switzerland: IUCN, 2002).

22. Fax and e-mails from Nigel Collar at BirdLife International, August 1993 and January 2002.

23. Diversity rankings and species counts from R.A. Mittermeier, P. Robles Gil, and C.G. Mittermeier, eds., *Megadiversity: Earth's Biologically Wealthiest Nations* (Monterey, Mexico: CEMEX, 1998). Threatened species rankings from Stattersfield and Capper, op. cit. note 5.

24. Collar, op. cit. note 22; Alison J. Stattersfield, Michael J. Crosby, Adrian J. Long, and David C. Wege, *Endemic Bird Areas of the World: Priorities for Biodiversity Conservation* (Cambridge: BirdLife International, 1998), pp. 21 and 30.

25. "New Owl Species in Sri Lanka," *World Birdwatch*, June 2001.

Habitat Loss: The Greatest Threat

1. John P. McCarty, "Ecological Consequences of Recent Climate Change," *Conservation Biology*, April 2001, pp. 320–9.

2. Alison J. Stattersfield and David R. Capper, eds., *Threatened Birds of the World* (Barcelona: Lynx Edicions, 2000), p. 8.

3. Janet Abramovitz, "Sustaining the World's Forests," *State of the World 1998* (New York: W.W. Norton & Company, 1998), pp. 21–2; D. Bryant, D. Nielson, and L. Tangley, *The Last Frontier Forests: Ecosystems and Economies on the Edge* (Washington, D.C.: World Resources Institute, 1997).

4. World Resources Institute, *World Resources 2000–2001* (Washington, D.C.: 2000), p. 90.

5. Stattersfield and Capper, op. cit. note 2.

6. "Temperate Woodland Gains," *Oryx*, vol. 33, no. 2, p. 989.

7. "Environmental Groups Demand Immediate Moratorium on New Chip Mills," press release from the Southern Environmental Law Center, April 25, 2000; Deborah Schoch, "Mistaking Trees for a Forest?," *Los Angeles Times*, May 23, 2002; Sue Anne Pressley, "Report Predicts Major Forest Loss in South," *Washington Post*, November 28, 2001.

8. Robert A. Askins, *Restoring North America's Birds* (New Haven and London: Yale University Press, 2000), pp. 138–43.

9. Ibid., pp. 26–53.

10. David S. Wilcove, *The Condor's Shadow* (New York: W.H. Freeman and Company, 1999), pp. 78–80.

11. William Stolzenburg, "Ghost Birds of the Grasslands," *Nature Conservancy*, Summer 2002, pp. 20–7.

12. Pete Gober and Mike Lockhart, "As Goes the Prairie Dog...So Goes the Ferret," *Endangered Species Bulletin*, vol. 21, no. 6 (November/December 1996), pp. 4, 5.

13. Heather J. Robertson and Richard G. Jefferson, "Nature and Farming in Britain," in Dana L. Jackson and Laura L. Jackson, *The Farm as Natural Habitat* (Washington, D.C.: Island Press, 2002), pp. 123–35.

14. Zoltán Waliczky, "Habitats for Birds in Europe," *World Birdwatch*, September 1997, pp. 16–9; BirdLife International website at www.birdlife.net/news, viewed November 2002.

15. World Resources Institute, op. cit. note 4, p. 122.

16. Amy Jansen and Alistar I. Robertson, "Riparian Bird Communities in Relation to Land Management Practices in Floodplain Woodlands of Southeastern Australia," *Biological Conservation* 100 (2001), pp. 173–85.

17. Stattersfield and Capper, op. cit. note 2, pp. 186–7 and 642–3.

18. World Resources Institute, op. cit. note 4, p. 104; Cosme Morillo and César Gómez-Campo, "Conservation in Spain, 1980–2000," *Biological Conservation*, vol. 95 (2000), p. 170.

19. Everglades conservation challenges from World Resources Institute, op. cit. note 4, p. 168–75; Doñana park from WWF website at www.panda.org/europe/donana/, viewed January 2002.

20. World Resources Institute, op. cit. note 4, p. 171, citing J.C. Ogden, "A Comparison of Wading Bird Nesting Colony Dynamics (1931–1946 and 1974–1989) as an Indication of Ecosystem Conditions in the Southern Everglades," in S.M. Davis and J.C. Ogden, *Everglades: The Ecosystem and Its Restoration* (Delray Beach, Florida: St. Lucie Press, 1994), and J.C. Ogden, "Status of Wading Bird Recovery, 1999," *South Florida Wading Bird Report*, vol. 5, no. 1, 1999.

21. Luba V. Balian, Mamikon G. Ghasabian, Martin S. Adamian, and Daniel Klem, Jr., "Changes in the Waterbird Community of the Lake Sevan-Lake Gilli Area, Republic of Armenia: A Case for Restoration," *Biological Conservation*, vol. 106, no. 2 (2002), pp. 157–63.

22. Andy J. Green, Mustapha El Hamzaoui, Mohammed Aziz El Agbani, and Jacques Franchimont, "The Conservation Status of Moroccan Wetlands With Particular Reference to Waterbirds and to Changes since 1978," *Biological Conservation*, vol. 104, no. 1 (2002), pp. 71–82.

23. Gonzalo Torreorgaz, "SEO/BirdLife, con apoyo de la UE, Ayudará Marruecos a que Gestione Sus Humedales," *Quercus*, vol. 202, December 2002, p. 10.

24. Scott Weidensaul, *Living on the Wind: Across the Hemisphere With Migrating Birds* (New York: North Point Press, 1999); Mary Deinlein, "Travel Alert for Migratory Birds: Stopover Sites in Decline," the Smithsonian Migratory Bird Center, at natzoo.si.edu/smbc/fxshts/fxsht6.htm, viewed May 2001; "Herons, Egrets, and Fish Ponds in Hong Kong," *Oryx*, vol. 33, no. 1 (1999), p. 14; Brett A. Lane, *Shorebirds in Australia* (Melbourne: Nelson Publishers, 1987), pp. 2–9.

25. Weidensaul, op. cit. note 24, pp. 105–25 and 334.

26. William Stolzenburg, "Raptor-rich Talamanca," *Nature Conservancy*, Summer 2002, p. 13.

27. Weidensaul, op. cit. note 24, pp. 243–6.

28. Peter P. Marra, Keith A. Hobson, and Richard T. Holmes, "Linking Winter and Summer Events in Migratory Birds by Using Stable-carbon Isotopes," *Science*, December 4, 1998, pp. 1884–1886; "Winter Is Key to Songbird Breeding Success," Environmental News Network, December 8, 1998, at www.enn.com/news/enn-stories/1998/ 12/120898/songbird.asp, viewed March 1999.

29. Wang Yong, Deborah M. Finch, Frank R. Moore, and Jeffrey F. Kelly, "Stopover Ecology and Habitat Use of Migratory Wilson's Warblers," *The Auk*, vol. 115, no. 4 (1998), pp. 829–42.

30. John Terborgh, *Where Have All the Birds Gone?* (Princeton: Princeton University Press, 1989), p. 95 and pp. 146–147; *Field Guide to the Birds of North America* (Washington, D.C.: National Geographic Society, 1999), pp. 302, 303; F. Gary Stiles and Alexander F. Skutch, *A Guide to the Birds of Costa Rica* (Ithaca, New York: Cornell University Press, 1989), p. 306.

31. Alison J. Stattersfield, Michael J. Crosby, Adrian J. Long, and David C. Wege, *Endemic Bird Areas of the World: Priorities for Biodiversity Conservation* (Cambridge: BirdLife International, 1998), pp. 400–5 and p. 27.

32. Gary K. Meffe and C. Ronald Carroll, *Principles of Conservation Biology* (Sunderland, Massachusetts: Sinauer Associates, Inc., 1997), pp. 276–302.

33. Ibid.

34. William F. Laurance, Susan G. Laurance, Leandro V. Ferreira, Judy M. Rankin-de Merona, Claude Gascon, and Thomas E. Lovejoy, "Biomass Collapse in Amazonian Forest Fragments," *Science*, November 7, 1997, pp. 1117–8.

35. Peter T. Fauth, "Reproductive Success of Wood Thrushes in Forest Fragments in Northern Indiana," *The Auk*, vol. 117, no. 1 (2000), pp. 194–204; Cheryl L. Trine, "Wood Thrush Population Sinks and Implications for the Scale of Regional Conservation Strategies," *Conservation Biology*, vol. 12, no. 3 (June 1998), pp. 576–85; David Ward and James N. M. Smith, "Brown-headed Cowbird Parasitism Results in a Sink Population in Warbling Vireos," *The Auk*, vol. 117, no. 2 (2000), pp. 337–44.

36. Hugh A. Ford, Geoffrey W. Barrett, Denis A. Saunders, and Harry F. Recher, "Why Have Birds in the Woodlands of Southern Australia Declined?" *Biological Conservation*, vol. 97 (2001), pp. 71–88; Richard E. Major, Fiona J. Christie, and Greg Gowing, "Influence of Remnant and Landscape Attributes on Australian Woodland Bird Communities," *Biological Conservation*, vol. 102, no. 1 (2001), pp. 47–66.

37. Yosihiro Natuhara and Chobei Imai, "Prediction of Species Richness of Breeding Birds by Landscape-level Factors of Urban Woods in Osaka Prefecture, Japan," *Biodiversity and Conservation* 8 (1999), pp. 239–53.

38. Richard T.T. Forman and Lauren E. Alexander, "Roads and Their Major Ecological Effects," *Annual Review of Ecological Systems*, 29 (1998), pp. 207–31.

39. Juan L. Bouzat, "The Population Genetic Structure of the Greater Rhea in an Agricultural Landscape," *Biological Conservation*, vol. 99, no. 3 (2001), pp. 277–84.

40. Juan L. Bouzat, Han H. Cheng, Harris A. Lewin, Ronald L. Westemeier, Jeffrey D. Brawn, and Ken N. Paige, "Genetic Evaluation of a Demographic Bottleneck in the Greater Prairie Chicken," *Conservation Biology*, vol. 12, no. 4 (1998), pp. 836–43.

41. J. Christopher Haney, "A Half-century Comparison of Breeding Birds in the Southern Appalachians," *The Condor*, vol. 103, pp. 268–77.

Alien Attacks

1. Invasive Species Specialist Group, "100 of the World's Worst Invasive Alien Species," at www.iucn.org/biodiversityday/100booklet.pdf, viewed January 2002.

2. Alison J. Stattersfield and David R. Capper, eds., *Threatened Birds of the World* (Barcelona: Lynx Edicions, 2000), p. 8.

3. Thomas Brooks, "Extinct Species," in Stattersfield and Capper, ibid., pp. 701–8; Stattersfield and Capper, op. cit. note 2, p. 8.

4. Chris Bright, *Life Out of Bounds* (New York: W.W. Norton & Company, 1998), pp. 114–8; Stattersfield and Capper, op. cit. note 2, pp. 174 and 706; William Claiborne, "Trouble in Paradise?: Serpentless Hawaii Fears Snake Invasion," *Washington Post*, August 23, 1997.

5. Stattersfield and Capper, op. cit. note 2, pp. 45–72.

6. D.J. Campbell and I.A.E. Atkinson, "Depression of Tree Recruitment by the Pacific Rat on New Zealand's Northern Offshore Islands," *Biological Conservation*, vol. 107, no. 1 (2002), pp. 19–35.

7. Alison J. Stattersfield, Michael J. Crosby, Adrian J. Long, and David C. Wege, *Endemic Bird Areas of the World: Priorities for Biodiversity Conservation* (Cambridge: BirdLife International, 1998), pp.154–67.

8. "Okinawa Rails in Peril," *World Birdwatch*, September 2001.

9. Brooks, op. cit. note 3, pp. 701–7.

10. Hugh A. Ford, Geoffrey W. Barrett, Denis A. Saunders, and Harry F. Recher, "Why Have Birds in the Woodlands of Southern Australia Declined?," *Biological Conservation*, vol. 97 (2001), pp. 79, 80, citing D.C. Paton, "Loss of Wildlife to Domestic Cats," in C. Potter (ed.), *The Impact of Cats on Native Wildlife* (Canberra: Australian National Parks and Wildlife Service, 1991), pp.

64–9, and D.C. Paton, "Impact of Domestic and Feral Cats on Wildlife," in G. Siepens and C. Owens (eds.), *Cat Management Workshop Proceedings* (Brisbane: Queensland Department of Environment and Heritage, 1993), pp. 9–15.

11. "Domestic Cat Predation on Birds and Other Wildlife," a report by the American Bird Conservancy at www.abcbirds.org/cats/catre/pdf, viewed May 2002. This source cites the University of Wisconsin cat study from J.S. Coleman and S.A. Temple, "How Many Birds Do Cats Kill?", *Wildlife Control Technology*: 44 (1995).

12. Stattersfield and Capper, op. cit. note 2, pp. 73, 300; Eric Dorfman, "Alien Invasives in the Tropical Pacific," *Wingspan*, vol. 11, no. 4 (2001), p. 23; Invasive Species Specialist Group, op. cit. note 1.

13. Stattersfield and Capper, op. cit. note 2, pp. 73, 300.

14. Invasive Species Specialist Group, op. cit. note 1; Stattersfield and Capper, op. cit. note 2, pp. 706–7.

15. Birgit Fessl and Sabine Tebbich, "*Philornis downsi*—A Recently Discovered Parasite on the Galapagos Archipelago—A Threat for Darwin's Finches?", *Ibis*, vol. 144 (2002), pp. 445–51; "Parasites Pose New Threat to Darwin's Finches," BirdLife International website at www.birdlife.net/news, viewed November 2002.

16. "Reports From the Workshop on Indian *Gyps* Vultures," a summary of recent studies presented at the fourth Eurasian Congress on Raptors in Seville, Spain in September 2001, from The National Birds of Prey Centre website at www.nbpc.co.uk/ivr2001.htm, viewed May 2002.

17. John H. Rappole, Scott R. Derrickson, and Zdenek Hubálek, "Migratory Birds and Spread of West Nile Virus in the Western Hemisphere," *Emerging Infectious Diseases* (Centers for Disease Control), vol. 6, no. 4 (July/August 2000), at www.cdc.gov/ncidod/eid/vol6no4/rappole.htm, viewed July 2002.

18. A. Green and B. Hughes, "Action Plan for the White-headed Duck in Europe," in *Globally Threatened Birds in Europe: Action Plans* (Strasbourg: Council of Europe Publishing, 1996), pp. 119–45.

19. "Tough Measures Against Invasive Ruddy Ducks," *World Birdwatch*, March 2002, p. 4.

20. Richard Manning, *Grassland: The History, Biology, Politics, and Promise of the American Prairie* (New York: Penguin Books, 1995), pp. 178–80; The Nature Conservancy's pest plant website at tncweeds.ucdavis.edu/esadocs/bromtect.html, viewed November 2002.

21. Kenn Kaufman, *Lives of North American Birds* (Boston: Houghton Mifflin, 1996), p. 153.

22. Bright, op. cit. note 4, p. 38.

23. Invasive Species Specialist Group, op. cit. note 1; Stephanie Flack and Elaine Furlow, "America's Least Wanted," *Nature Conservancy*, November/December 1996, p. 22.

24. George W. Cox, *Alien Species in North America: Impacts on Natural Ecosystems* (Washington, D.C.: Island Press, 1999), p. 178.

25. David M. Richardson, "Forestry Trees as Invasive Aliens," *Conservation Biology*, February 1998, pp. 18–25; Jim Hone, "Feral Pigs in Namadgi National Park, Australia: Dynamics, Impacts, and Management," *Biological Conservation*, vol. 105, no. 2 (2002), pp. 231–42.

26. D. Pimentel, L. Lach, R. Zuniga, and D. Morrison, "Environmental and Economic Costs Associated With Non-indigenous Species in the United States," *BioScience*, vol. 50, no. 1 (2000), pp. 53–65.

Exploitation: Hunting, Capture, and Fishing

1. Howard Youth, "The Killing Fields," *Wildlife Conservation*, July/August 1999, p. 16; BirdLife Malta website at www.birdlifemalta.org/, viewed October 2002.

2. BirdLife Malta, op. cit. note 1.

3. "5,317 Bird-Trapping Sites," *British Birds*, July 2001, p. 335; "Working To Change Attitutes," *World Birdwatch*, October 1999; "Dos Nuevos Informes Tratan de Impedir el 'Parany' en la Comunidad Valenciana," *La Garcilla*, no. 111 (2001), p. 33.

4. Buntings from "Widespread Hunting of 'Rice Birds' in China," *World Birdwatch*, September 2001, p. 8; "Migrating Birds Hunted in China," *Oryx*, vol. 33, no. 3 (1999), p. 203. Sparrows from Chris Buckley, "China's Sparrows Imperiled, Again," *International Herald Tribune*, April 4, 2002; *World Birdwatch*, December 2001, p. 3.

5. Josep del Hoyo, Andrew Elliott, and Jordi Sargatal, *Handbook of the Birds of the World, Volume 2* (Barcelona: Lynx Edicions, 1994), pp. 325–7 and 336–41.

6. Ibid., pp. 325–7, 336–41, and 533–50.

7. N. Snyder, P. McGowan, J. Gilardi, A. Grajal, eds., *Parrots: Status Survey and Conservation Action Plan* (Gland, Switzerland: IUCN, 1999).

8. The Ramsar Convention on Wetlands from www.ramsar.org/; MAB Program from www.unesco.org/mab/ about.htm; World Heritage Convention from whc.unesco.org/nwhc/pages/doc/main.htm; CITES from www.cites.org/eng /disc/what_is.shtml; the Convention on the Conservation of Migratory Species of Wild Animals from www.wcmc.org.uk/cms/intro.htm; Convention on Biodiversity from www.biodiv.org/.

9. Snyder et al., op. cit. note 7; Robert S. Ridgely and Paul J. Greenfield, *The Birds of Ecuador: Status, Distribution, and Taxonomy* (Ithaca, New York: Cornell University Press, 2001), p. 89.

10. Ridgely and Greenfield, op. cit. note 9.

11. TRAFFIC website at www.traffic.org, viewed December 2002.

12. Alison J. Stattersfield and David R. Capper, eds., *Threatened Birds of the World* (Barcelona: Lynx Edicions, 2000), pp. 545, 594.

13. "Longlining: A Major Threat to the World's Seabirds," *World Birdwatch*, June 2000, pp. 10–14; "Sudden Death on the High Seas," American Bird Conservancy report at www.abcbirds.org/policy/seabird_report.pdf , viewed June 2002; Stattersfield and Capper, op. cit. note 12, pp. 45–53.

14. Svein Løkkeborg and Graham Robertson, "Seabird and Longline Interactions: Effects of a Bird-scaring Streamer Line and Line Shooter on the Incidental Capture of Northern Fulmars," *Biological Conservation*, vol. 106, no. 3 (2002), pp. 359–64; E.J. Belda and A. Sánchez, "Seabird Mortality on Longline Fisheries in the Western Mediterranean: Factors Affecting Bycatch and Proposed Mitigating Measures," *Biological Conservation*, vol. 98, no. 3 (2001), pp. 357–63.

15. American Bird Conservancy, op. cit. note 13.

16. BirdLife International website at www.birdlife.org.uk/news, viewed October 2002; "Agreement on the Conservation of Albatrosses and Petrels" at the Environment Australia website at www.ea.gov.au/biodiversity/international/albatross/, viewed June 2002.

Chemical Threats

1. Susie Ellis, John P. Croxall, and John Cooper, eds., *Penguin Conservation Assessment and Management Plan*, a report on the September 1996 workshop in Cape Town, South Africa, organized by British Antarctic Survey, SCAR Bird Biology Subcommittee, Percy Fitzpatrick Institute of African Ornithology, and the Conservation Breeding Specialist Group of the IUCN/SSC (Apple Valley, Minnesota: IUCN/SSC, August 1998), pp. 8, 9.

2. Curtis Runyan and Magnar Norderhaug, "The Path to the Johannesburg Summit," *World Watch*, vol. 15, no. 3, May/June 2002, p. 33.

3. "Europe's Worst Ever Atlantic Coast Oil Spill Disaster," *World Birdwatch*, March 2000.

4. Donwald Pressly, "SA Hit by 10 Oil Spills in 12 Years," *The Sunday Times* (South Africa), November 10, 2002; "Race To Pump Oil Off SA Ship," BBC website at news.bbc.co.uk, viewed October 2002.

5. Bhushan Bahree, Carlta Vitzthum, and Erik Portanger, "Tanker Saga Illustrates How Rescues Are Hurt by Cross-Current Goals," *Wall Street Journal Europe*, November 25, 2002; Emma Daly, "Two Months After Oil Spill, Spain Is Still Struggling To Clean Up," *New York Times*, January 19, 2003.

6. "SEO/BirdLife Estima Que Ya Han Muerto Entre 10,000 y 15,000 Aves a Causa de la Marea Negra Originada por el *Prestige*. El Arao Común podría Extinguirse en España," at the SEO/BirdLife website at www.seo.org/2002/prestige/noticias.asp?id=126, viewed December 2002.

7. William Moskoff, "The Impact of Oil Spills on Birds," *Birding*, February 2000, pp. 44–9.

8. Juan Forero, "Ambitions Scaled Back for Ecuador Pipeline," *International Herald Tribune*, October 31, 2002; James V. Grimaldi, "Texas Firms Line Up U.S. Aid in Peru," *Washington Post*, November 20, 2002.

9. John P. McCarty and Anne L. Secord, "Possible Effects of PCB Contamination on Female Plumage Color and Reproductive Success in Hudson River Tree Swallows," *The Auk*, vol. 117, no. 4 (2000), pp. 987–95.

10. John P. McCarty and Anne L. Secord, "Nest-building Behavior in PCB-Contaminated Tree Swallows," *The Auk*, vol. 116, no. 1 (1999), pp. 55–63.

11. David Pimentel, et al., "Environmental and Economic Costs of Pesticide Use," *BioScience*, vol. 42, no. 10, (1992), pp. 750–60.

12. Humphrey Crick, "Poisoned Prey in the Heart of Africa," *New Scientist*, November 24, 1990, pp. 39–42.

13. Mary Deinlein, "When It Comes to Pesticides, Birds Are Sitting Ducks," Smithsonian Migratory Bird Center at natzoo.si.edu/smbc/fxshts/fxsht8.htm, viewed April 2001.

14. G.R. Potts, *The Partridge: Pesticides, Predation and Conservation* (London: Collins, 1986), cited in Dan E. Chamberlain and Humphrey Q.P. Crick, "Population Declines and Reproductive Performance of Skylarks in Different Regions and Habitats of the United Kingdom," *Ibis*, vol. 141 (1999), pp. 38–51.

15. Anne Platt McGinn, "Malaria, Mosquitoes, and DDT," *World Watch*, vol. 15, no. 3, May/June 2002, pp. 10–16; "WWF Efforts To Phase Out DDT," at WWF Global Toxics Initiative website at www.worldwildlife.org/toxics/progareas/pop/ddt.htm, viewed May 2002.

16. Deinlein, op. cit. note 13.

17. "Agreement Reached To Save Swainson's Hawks," press release from American Bird Conservancy, Washington, D.C., October 15, 1996; Santiago Krapovickas, "Swainson's Hawk in Argentina: International Crisis and Cooperation," *World Birdwatch*, December 1997; "Swainson's Hawk Recovery," *World Birdwatch*, March 1997.

18. *World Birdwatch*, March and December 1997, op. cit. note 17.

19. International Programme on Chemical Safety/INCHEM website at www.inchem.org/, viewed October 2002.

20. American Bird Conservancy, Defenders of Wildlife, and Florida Wildlife Federation, "Groups Sue EPA To Protect Florida Wildlife From Bird-killing Pesticide," press release (Washington, D.C.: October 28, 2002).

21. Potts, op. cit. note 14.

22. J. Hellmich, "Impacto del Uso de Pesticidas Sobre Las Aves: El Caso de la Avutarda," *Ardeola*, vol. 39, no. 2 (1992), pp. 7–22.

23. "Service Continues To Expand Non-toxic Shot Options—Study Shows Ban on Lead Shot Saves Millions of Waterfowl," U.S. Fish & Wildlife Service press release, October 25, 2000, at southeast.fws.gov/news/2000/r00-045.html.

24. Lead Shot Ban Throughout Sweden," *Oryx*, vol. 33, no. 3 (1999), p. 198.

25. U.S. Fish & Wildlife Service, op. cit. note 23.

26. A. Acosta, "El Gobierno Prohíbe la Caza y el Tiro con Plomo en los Humedales Españoles," *ABC*, May 31, 2001, p. 36; "El Plomo se Aleja de las Aves," *Biológica*, November 2001, p. 9.

27. Steve Nadis, "Getting the Lead Out," *National Wildlife*, August/September 2001, pp. 46–50; "EPA To Ban Lead Fishing Sinkers," *EDF Letter*, vol. 24, no. 5, September 1993; "State Acts for Loons," *Oryx*, vol. 33, no. 4, 1999, pp. 285–93.

28. José Antonio Montero, "Castilla y León Cierra Dos Cotos en los que se Halló Fauna Envenenada," *Quercus*, vol. 190, December 2001, p. 64.

29. A. Acosta, "El Censo del Águila Imperial Revela un Leve pero Constante Aumento de su Población," *ABC*, January 13, 2003.

Other Hazards of a Humanized World

1.   Guyonne F.E. Janss, "Avian Mortality From Power Lines: A Morphologic Approach of a Species-specific Mortality," *Biological Conservation*, vol. 95, no. 3 (2000), pp. 353–9; "Entre Ondas Electromagnéticas," *Biológica*, June 2002, p. 12.

2.   Juan C. Alonso, Javier A. Alonso, and Rodrigo Muñoz-Pulido, "Mitigation of Bird Collisions With Transmission Lines Through Groundwire Marking," *Biological Conservation*, vol. 67 (1994), pp. 129–34; Kjetil Bevanger and Henrik Brøseth, "Bird Collisions With Power Lines—An Experiment With Ptarmigan," *Biological Conservation*, vol. 99, no. 3 (2001), pp. 341–6.

3. "Environmental Groups File Petition Demanding Halt to All Construction of Communication Towers in Gulf Coast—Say Threat to Birds Must Be Addressed," press release (Washington, D.C.: American Bird Conservancy and Forest Conservation Council, August 28, 2002).

4. Towerkill.com website, "U.S.A. Towerkill Summary," at www.towerkill.com/issues/consum.html, viewed March 2002; Wendy K. Weisensel, "Battered by Airwaves?," *Wisconsin Natural Resources*, February 2000, at www.wnrmag.com/stories/2000/feb00/birdtower.htm, viewed March 2002.

5. "U.S.A. Towerkill Summary" and Weisensel, op. cit. note 4, based on U.S. Federal Aviation Administration figures.

6. Maureen F. Harvey, "Proposed Windfarms Equal Potential Threats to Migrating Songbirds and Raptors," *The Maryland Yellowthroat*, January/February 2003, pp. 5, 6.

7. Marlise Simons, "Converting Wind Energy Into Big Business," *International Herald Tribune*, December 9, 2002.

8. "El Impacto de los Molinos Navarros," *Quercus*, vol. 202, p. 66.

9. John P. McCarty, "Ecological Consequences of Recent Climate Change," *Conservation Biology*, April 2001, pp. 320–9; Jeff Price and Patricia Glick, *The Birdwatcher's Guide to Global Warming*, (Washington, D.C.: American Bird Conservancy and National Wildlife Federation, 2002), p. 3.

10. McCarty, op. cit. note 9; Price and Glick, op. cit. note 9; Mones S. Abu-Asab, Paul M. Peterson, Stanwyn G. Shetler, and Sylvia S. Orli, "Earlier Plant Flowering in Spring as a Response to Global Warming in the Washington, D.C., Area," *Biodiversity and Conservation* 10 (2001), pp. 597–612; Alvin Breisch and James Gibbs, "Climate Warming and Calling Phenology of Frogs Near Ithaca, New York, 1900–1999," *Conservation Biology*, 15 (August 2001), pp. 1175–8; Chris Bright, *Life Out of Bounds* (New York: W.W. Norton & Company, 1998), pp. 191–4.

11. "Global Warming a Threat to Long-distance Migrants," *World Birdwatch*, vol. 23, no. 3, September 2001, p. 5, citing a report in *Nature* (411:296–298).

12. Price and Glick, op. cit. note 9, pp. 9, 21.

13. Christoph Zockler and Igor Lysenko, "Water Birds on the Edge: Impact Assessment of Climate Change on Arctic-breeding Water Birds," an executive summary on the Biodiversity and Climate Change webpage of the United Nations Environment Programme and World Conservation Monitoring Center at unep-wcmc.org/climate/waterbirds/executive.htm, viewed March 2002.

14. Price and Glick, op. cit. note 9, pp. 18–21.

15. "Galapagos Penguins Under Threat," *World Birdwatch*, December 1998; Alison J. Stattersfield and David R. Capper, eds., *Threatened Birds of the World* (Barcelona: Lynx Edicions, 2000), p. 43.

16. Glen Martin, "The Case of the Disappearing Ducks," *National Wildlife*, April/May 2002.

17. Gary K. Meffe and C. Ronald Carroll, *Principles of Conservation Biology* (Sunderland, Massachusetts: Sinauer Associates, Inc., 1997), p. 299; George W. Cox, *Alien Species in North America and Hawaii: Impacts on Natural Ecosystems* (Washington, D.C.: Island Press, 1999), pp. 310–1; L. Hannah, G.F. Midgley, T. Lovejoy, W.J. Bond, M. Bush, J.C. Lovett, D. Scott, and F.I. Woodward, "Conservation of Biodiversity in a Changing Climate," *Conservation Biology*, vol. 16, no. 1 (February 2002), pp. 264–8.

Putting Back the Pieces...and Nature's Response

1.   Alison J. Stattersfield and David R. Capper, eds., *Threatened Birds of the World* (Barcelona: Lynx Edicions, 2000), p. 453.

2.   "The Peregrine Falcon Is Back: Babbitt Announces Removal of World's Fastest Bird From Endangered Species List," press release, (Washington, D.C.: U.S. Fish & Wildlife Service, August 20, 1999).

3.   "The Bald Eagle Is Back," press release (Washington, D.C.: U.S. Fish & Wildlife Service, July 2, 1999).

4.   Ted Williams, "Wanted: More Hunters," *Audubon*, March/April 2002, pp. 43–51.

5.   Meredith W. Cornett, Lee E. Frelich, Klaus J. Puettmann and Peter B. Reich, "Conservation Implications of Browsing by *Odocoileus virginianus* in Remnant Upland *Thuja occidentalis* Forests," *Biological Conservation*, vol. 93, no. 3 (2000), pp. 359–69; J. Darl Fletcher, Lisa A. Shipley, William J. McShea, and Durland L. Shumway, "Wildlife Herbivory and Rare Plants: The Effects of White-tailed Deer, Rodents, and Insects on Growth and Survival of Turk's Cap Lily," *Biological Conservation*, vol. 101, no. 2 (2001), pp. 229–38.

6. Williams, op. cit. note 4.

7.   "Japanese Stilt Grass," at National Park Service website at www.nps.gov/plants/alien/fact/mivi1.htm and e-mail from naturalist Suzanne Malone, Huntley Meadows Park, Virginia, April 2000.

8.   St. Johns River Water Management District, "Program Overview: Lake Apopka Basin," at sjr.state.fl.us/programs/acq_restoration/s_water/lapopka /overview.html, viewed November 2002; e-mails from Bill Pranty, Audubon of Florida, and Gian Basili, St. Johns River Water Management District, February 2002.

9. "Lab Results Released From Lake Apopka Wildlife Death Investigation," press release (Washington, D.C.: U.S. Fish & Wildlife Service, June 11, 2001); e-mail from Gian Basili, St. Johns River Water Management District, December 2002.

10. Basili, op. cit. note 9.

Taking Stock

1. R.D. Gregory et al., "The Population Status of Birds in the U.K.," *British Birds*, vol. 95 (2002), p. 421; Mark Cocker, "Future Challenges in Africa," *Birding*, June 2002, pp. 262–4.

2. Michael A. Patten and Curtis A. Marantz, "Implications of Vagrant Southeastern Vireos and Warblers in California," *The Auk*, vol. 113, no. 4 (1996), pp. 911–23.

3. Alison J. Stattersfield, BirdLife International, e-mail, June 2002.

4. Ibid., and L.D.C. Fishpool and Michael I. Evans, eds., *Important Bird Areas in Africa and Its Associated Islands: Priority Sites for Conservation* (Newbury and Cambridge, U.K.: NatureBureau and BirdLife International, 2001); Melanie F. Heath, Michael I. Evans, D.G. Hoccom, A.J. Payne, and N.B. Peet, eds., *Important Bird Areas in Europe: Priority Sites for Conservation* (Cambridge, U.K.: BirdLife International, 2001); Nigel J. Collar, A.V. Andreev, S. Chan, M.J. Crosby, S. Subramanya, and J.A. Tobias, eds., *Threatened Birds of Asia: The BirdLife International Red Data Book* (Cambridge, U.K.: BirdLife International, 2001).

5. Alison J. Stattersfield, Michael J. Crosby, Adrian J. Long, and David C. Wege, *Endemic Bird Areas of the World: Priorities for Biodiversity Conservation* (Cambridge: BirdLife International, 1998), p. 29.

6. Frank Gill, et al., *American Birds: Ninety-ninth Christmas Bird Count (CBC)* (New York: National Audubon Society, 1999); U.S. Geological Survey CBC introduction at www.mp1-pwrc.usgs.gov/birds/cbc.html#intro , viewed April 2002; 101st CBC summary at www.audubon.org/bird/cbc/101stsummary.html, viewed April 2002.

7. Asian Waterbird Census website at www.wetlands.agro.nl/wetlands_icu /ap/inf2000.doc, viewed May 2002.

8. Other citizen science projects from www.birdsource.org, viewed May 2002.

9. Chris Tzaros, "Swift Flight to Recovery," *Wingspan*, June 2002, pp. 8–11.

Conservation Strategies and Priorities

1. Gary K. Meffe and C. Ronald Carroll, *Principles of Conservation Biology* (Sunderland, Massachusetts: Sinauer Associates, Inc., 1997), pp. 7–21.

2. Mark Cheater, "Saving the Wrong Places?", *National Wildlife*, August/September 2001, p. 10.

3. Andrew Hansen and Jay Rotella, "Biophysical Factors, Land Use, and Species Viability In and Around Nature Reserves," *Conservation Biology*, vol. 16, no. 4, August 2002, pp. 1–12.

4. Alison J. Stattersfield, Michael J. Crosby, Adrian J. Long, and David C. Wege, *Endemic Bird Areas of the World: Priorities for Biodiversity Conservation* (Cambridge: BirdLife International, 1998), pp. 270–2.

5. World Resources Institute, *World Resources 2000–2001* (Washington, D.C., 2000), p. 244. Larger figure, 8.8 percent, from M.J.B. Green and J.R. Paine, "State of the World's Protected Areas at the End of the Twentieth Century," presented at the IUCN World Commission on Protected Areas Symposium at Albany, Australia, November 1997, at www.wcmc.org.uk/protected_areas/albany.htm, viewed January 2002. This figure includes marine reserves.

6. Mark Jolly, "Lands of Opportunity," *Nature Conservancy*, Winter 2002, pp. 32–43; David Dobbs, "Locking Up Your Land," *Audubon*, December 2002, pp. 100–2.

7. Richard L. Knight, "Private Lands: The Neglected Geography," *Conservation Biology*, vol. 13, no. 2, April 1999, pp. 223, 224; Catherine M. Allen and Stephen R. Edwards, "The Sustainable-Use Debate: Observations From IUCN," *Oryx*, vol. 29, no. 2, April 1995, pp. 92–8.

8. Jeffrey A. McNeely and Sara J. Scherr, *Common Ground, Common Future: How Ecoagriculture Can Help Feed the World and Save Wild Biodiversity*, a report commissioned by Future Harvest, based on a study commissioned by IUCN—The World Conservation Union; available at www.futureharvest.org/pdf/biodiversity_report.pdf, viewed July 2002.

9. Robert A. Rice and Justin R. Ward, *Coffee, Conservation, and Commerce in the Western Hemisphere* (Washington, D.C.: Smithsonian Migratory Bird Center and Natural Resources Defense Council, June 1996); Lisa J. Petit, "Shade-grown Coffee: It's for the Birds," *Endangered Species Bulletin*, July/August 1998, pp. 14, 15; "Why Your Daily Fix Can Fix More Than Your Head," Brian Halweil, *World Watch*, vol. 15, no. 3, May/June 2002, pp. 36–40.

10. Malcolm Smith, "Spanish Sorcery," *BBC Wildlife*, March 2001, pp. 64–7; Cacao, IPM, and organic farming from mission statement for 1998 sustainable cacao conference, Smithsonian Migratory Bird Center and Smithsonian Tropical Research Institute, Panama City, Panama, March 30, 1998, at natzoo.si.edu/smbc/Research/Cacao/cacaomission.htm, viewed February 2002;

"The Biodiversity Benefits of Organic Farming," a Soil Association briefing paper dated May 27, 2000, at www.soilassociation.org/, viewed April 2002.

11. United States Department of Agriculture, "USDA Commits Historic Resources to Conservation on Private Working Lands," press release (Washington, D.C., June 3, 2002); phone call from Wayne Baggett, USDA, January 22, 2003.

12. "The Conservation Reserve Program," United States Department of Agriculture, Farm Service Agency, PA-1603, revised October 2001; Tina Adler, "Prairie Tales: What Happens When Farmers Turn Prairies Into Farmland and Farmland Into Prairies," *Science News*, vol. 149, January 20, 1996, pp. 44, 45; Dan L. Reinking, "A Closer Look: Henslow's Sparrow," *Birding*, vol. 34, no. 2, April 2002, pp. 146–53, citing J.R. Herkert, "Population Trends of the Henslow's Sparrow in Relation to the Conservation Reserve Program in Illinois, 1975–1995," *Journal of Field Ornithology*, 68, pp. 235–44.

13. C.J.M. Musters, M. Kruk, H.J. De Graaf, and W.J. Ter Keurs, "Breeding Birds as a Farm Product," *Conservation Biology*, April 2001, pp. 363–9.

14. C.J.M. Musters, Environmental Biology Institute of Evolutionary and Ecological Sciences, Leiden University, The Netherlands, e-mail to author, May 2002.

15. Martha Honey, *Ecotourism and Sustainable Development: Who Owns Paradise?* (Washington, D.C.: Island Press, 1999), pp. 3–25.

16. Duan Biggs, BirdLife South Africa project coordinator, e-mail to author, August 2002; Stephen W. Evans, "Blue Swallow Action Plan Workshop," BirdLife South Africa, at www.birdlife.org.za, viewed August 2002.

17. Biggs, op. cit. note 16; Evans, op. cit. note 16.

18. William Shepard, "Birding Trails in North America," *Birding*, vol. 33, no. 5 (2001), pp. 416–27; "Birding Florida on the Great Birding Trail," www.florida birdingtrail.com, viewed April 2002.

19. Shepard, op. cit. note 18; Jennifer Bogo, "Backseat Birder," *Audubon*, September 2002, pp. 61, 62.

20. U.S. Department of Interior and U.S. Department of Commerce, *2001 National Survey of Fishing, Hunting, and Wildlife-Associated Recreation: Survey Highlights*; federalaid.fws.gov/surveys/surveys.html, viewed October 2002.

21. H. Ken Cordell and Nancy G. Herbert, "The Popularity of Birding Is Still Growing," *Birding*, vol. 34, no. 1 (2002), pp. 54–61.

22. Interview with Juan Carlos Alonso, CSIC biologist, Madrid, Spain, October 2002.

23. Ibid.

24. Ibid.

25. Juliette Jowit, "Pragmatism Is for the Birds," *Financial Times*, September 13, 2001.

26. Vanessa Kauffman, Wildlife Habitat Council, e-mails to author, December 2002.

27. Ibid.

28. Chris Eberly, "Defending the Steppingstones of Migration," *Birding*, October 2002, pp. 450–8.

29. Courtney Leatherman, "Central American Countries United To Protect the "Path of the Panther," *Nature Conservancy*, summer 2002, p. 55; e-mail from Jim Barborak, Wildlife Conservation Society, January 2003.

30. F.L. Filion, "Birds as a Socio-economic Resource: A Strategic Concept in Promoting Conservation," in A.W. Diamond and F.L. Filion, *The Value of Birds* (Cambridge: International Council for Bird Preservation, 1987), p. 8.

Index